W9-ARB-130

The Future of Money
in the
Information Age

WITHDRAWN

WITHDRAWN

The Future of Money
in the
Information Age

Edited by James A. Dorn

CATO
INSTITUTE
Washington, D.C.

Copyright © 1997 by the Cato Institute.
All rights reserved.

Library of Congress Cataloging-in-Publication Data

The future of money in the information age / edited by James A. Dorn
    p.   cm.
    A collection of original articles by various authors.
    Includes bibliographical references and index.
    ISBN 1-882577-52-3 (paper)
    1. Money.   2. Electronic funds transfers.   3. Monetary policy.
I. Dorn, James A.
HG221.F888   1997
332.4′0285—dc21   97-686
                                                          CIP

CATO INSTITUTE
1000 Massachusetts Ave., N.W.
Washington, D.C. 20001

CONTENTS

PREFACE

The information revolution has narrowed space and time but has broadened freedom and commerce. Gold was once the dominant medium of exchange, then came paper money, and now electronic cash is a reality. The basis of the new monetary universe is sand rather than paper—a computer chip rather than a Federal Reserve note. The advent of e-money offers the possibility of privatizing the supply of currency, paying interest on small deposits, and making offshore banking accessible to many individuals. In the future, government fiat money may disappear as people choose to hold digital money issued by private firms rather than non-interest-bearing paper money issued by central banks.

The essays in this book consider the implications of the information revolution for financial innovation and the future of money. Within that broad framework, contributors examine the regulatory climate; the impact of e-money on taxation, banking, and monetary policy; and the problem of maintaining privacy in the new monetary universe. All of the papers, except those by Alan Greenspan and Lawrence Gasman, were first presented at the Cato Institute's 14th annual Monetary Conference, "The Future of Money in the Information Age," which was held in Washington, D.C., on May 23, 1996.

Several acknowledgments are in order. First, I would like to thank Corporate One, E*Trade Securities, Inc., and *Forbes ASAP* for helping sponsor the 14th annual Monetary Conference. Their financial and other assistance is greatly appreciated. Next, I thank all the contributors for their diligence in preparing their papers for publication; several of the conference papers were substantially revised for this volume. Finally, I thank my colleagues Ed Crane, David Boaz, and Jacobo Rodriguez: Ed for his ongoing support of basic monetary research, David for suggesting the conference topic, and Jacobo for his assistance from start to finish.

James A. Dorn

1

INTRODUCTION
THE FUTURE OF MONEY
James A. Dorn

> Just as fiat money replaced specie-backed paper currencies, electronically initiated debits and credits will become the dominant payment modes, creating the potential for private money to compete with government-issued currencies.
>
> —Jerry L. Jordan

Transition to a New Monetary Universe

Money is a social convention, a widely accepted medium of exchange, a store of value, and a unit of account. Sound money is essential for a smoothly functioning market system. Wide swings in the value of money distort the information contained in relative prices and misdirect the flow of resources. The wealth of the nation declines as a result. Moreover, the absence of monetary stability causes people to lose confidence in the monetary system and, at the same time, provides government with the incentive to impose wage and price controls, which further distort markets and impair individual freedom.

There is a certain inertia in the current U.S. fiat money regime: even though persistent inflation has eroded the value of the dollar over the past 50 years, so that a 1947 dollar is now worth only 14 cents, most people continue to hold the Federal Reserve System in high esteem. In the future, however, government fiat money may be placed on the endangered species list as people shift from paper currency to electronic cash (e-cash). Stored-value cards ("smart

---

James A. Dorn is Vice President for Academic Affairs at the Cato Institute and Professor of Economics at Towson State University.

cards" with an embedded micro chip that stores money in digital form) may become a customary circulating medium along with privately supplied digital cash stored in computer hard drives and used over the Internet to facilitate electronic commerce.

The transition from a paper-based monetary system to an electronic payments system will reduce transactions costs, expand markets, and empower individuals. The speed of that transition and the expected benefits, however, will depend on creating a legal infrastructure that penalizes failure and rewards success. The rules that govern the new monetary universe will have to be transparent, equally applied, and consistent with individual freedom if people are to have trust and confidence in cybermoney and cybercommerce.

The more basic issue, of course, is what type of monetary institutions are consistent with monetary freedom and monetary stability? The Greenspan Fed has done a good job of combating inflation, but what is to prevent a future Fed chairman from pursuing targets other than price stability and eroding the future value of money? High and variable inflation can lead to a controlled economy and destroy the price system. That is why it is so important to think clearly about alternative monetary regimes and to select those that offer the best protection for private property and personal freedom. The advent of private e-money and the end of the Fed's monopoly over currency will increase monetary freedom and could lead to a new monetary standard.

Thus far, the Fed is generally supportive of monetary innovation. Federal Reserve Board governor Edward W. Kelley Jr., for example, sees "private-sector experimentation with new payment and banking products" as "a positive development." And he recognizes that "direct competition between the Federal Reserve . . . and the private sector could well stifle the current climate of innovation" (Kelley 1996: 9).

The papers in this volume examine the changing nature of money and banking in the information age; consider the implications of e-money for monetary control, taxation, and regulation (If money can be encrypted, can government control it, tax it, and regulate it?); and address the question of who should be allowed to issue e-money. Underpinning the entire discussion is the problem of privacy and the role of government in the new monetary universe.

Electronic Commerce and Monetary Evolution

The papers in Part I point to the evolutionary character of the payments system and consider how e-money may develop in light of new technology and changing domains of trust. The myriad implications of those changes for policy and freedom are touched upon.

In chapter 2, **Lawrence H. White**, a University of Georgia economist specializing in monetary history, traces how technological changes have affected the payments system, making it possible to move from what he calls "analog currency" (paper bank notes and coins) to digital currency. If issuers of digital currency were to pay interest and safeguard privacy, argues White, the public would have a strong incentive to shift from government fiat money to privately issued e-cash. Ending the government's currency monopoly, however, would not necessarily change the monetary standard: digital currency would be convertible into U.S. dollars, and those dollars would be fiat money. Moreover, according to White, the Federal Reserve could still control monetary aggregates by controlling the monetary base, which would consist solely of bank reserves.

For White, the most promising benefit of the transition to a secure and inexpensive electronic payments system is the potential it offers for offshore banking. He predicts that "when commercial on-line networks and Internet sites begin offering offshore banking services, with zero or very small fees for transferring funds, an exodus of retail banking business will begin from the regulated onshore sector to the untaxed and unregulated offshore sector."

William Melton, founder of CyberCash, focuses on the concept of electronic liquidity and the importance of trust in chapter 3. "Liquidity," he writes, "can only be produced from a domain of trust." Two domains are pertinent: "a domain of actuarial trust" (often found in a market system) and "a domain of guaranteed trust" (found in hierarchical structures). In the first domain, trust is generated by feedback from statistical tracking and in the second, by an "external guarantor." Melton sees technological advances in cryptography creating greater trust and efficiency in the electronic payments system and enabling financial markets to provide greater liquidity. The increased liquidity, however, need not be inflationary—if it "is provided under the tight feedback loops of the market." In other words, the information revolution will create more liquidity (trust) and more markets. Melton is therefore optimistic that we are entering "a new age of plenty and opportunity."

Bill Frezza, president of Wireless Computing Associates, is also optimistic. In chapter 4, he predicts an era of increased liberty as individuals use the Internet to globalize money and commerce and to end the government's monetary sovereignty. He envisions an enlarged private sphere in cyberspace, beyond the reach of government, in which "sovereign individuals will have the tools to construct a practical realization of laissez-faire capitalism." At the center of that space, writes Frezza, "will be new monetary institutions that must inherently rest on the consent of the participants."

In the final chapter of Part I, **Lawrence Gasman**, director of telecommunications and technology studies at the Cato Institute, considers the potential of the Internet, or World Wide Web, within the confines of existing technology. He asks whether the Internet, which is based on "a innovative combination of older technologies," is likely to end distance-based pricing and empower people to the extent claimed. Gasman expects Internet service providers to be able to charge by distance in the foreseeable future, and he expects a regulatory push in that direction. He agrees that the Web "offers a powerful new tool for entrepreneurs," provides consumers with greater freedom of choice, and makes e-cash and electronic banking feasible. But he does not see the end of government interference and a world dominated by small traders in cyberspace. Reality dictates that "the price of free commerce and free banking on the Net will be much the same as for freedom itself—namely, eternal vigilance."

Financial Innovation, Regulation, and Taxation

Financial innovation depends on experimentation and the freedom to fail, as well as the right to profit from success. Markets are driven by individuals who are willing to take risks in the search for new opportunities and profit. In the process of discovery, privately enforced informal rules often emerge that later become codified and enforced by government; the market typically leads the process of innovation, and government follows. The question thus becomes, what is the role of government in financial innovation? If overzealous regulators restrict experimentation and make the emerging electronic marketplace too costly, the development of e-cash will be nipped in the bud.

The papers in Part II deal with regulation, taxation, and privacy as they relate to the financial services revolution. How the Congress, the Federal Reserve, and the Treasury, in particular, view the transition to electronic cash and commerce will shape the future of the electronic payments system. A laissez-faire attitude will foster innovation; a protectionist attitude will mean that special interests will determine the pace of innovation and who captures the rewards and bears the costs. The challenge for government will be to provide a legal framework that safeguards property rights and expands markets so that wealth is created rather than destroyed.

The early signals are encouraging: regulatory agencies are taking a wait-and-see approach to financial innovation in cyberspace, although there is considerable concern about the impact of e-money on tax collection and on criminal activity.

In chapter 6, Federal Reserve Board chairman **Alan Greenspan** draws a lesson from the success of self-regulation during the "free-banking" era in 19th-century America: "If we wish to foster financial innovation, we must be careful not to impose rules that inhibit it." He emphasizes that, in the case of e-cash or the electronic payments system, "the private sector will need the flexibility to experiment, without broad interference by government."

Greenspan also draws on lessons learned from the Federal Reserve's role in developing the Automated Clearing House system to argue that government involvement in the design of new technology often deters private alternatives. The lesson for "electronic money and banking . . . is that consumers and merchants, not government, will ultimately determine what new products are successful in the marketplace. Government action can retard progress, but almost certainly cannot ensure it."

In chapter 7, **Scott Cook**, chairman of Intuit, examines the forces behind the financial services revolution. He begins by looking at the increased complexity consumers face when choosing financial instruments and the trend toward greater self-reliance. In his view, the Internet is ideally suited to deal with both issues. Another trend is the movement toward greater freedom in the provision of financial services as the industry is deregulated. That trend will allow the industry to serve consumers better as they deal with complexity and strive for greater autonomy in planning their financial future. Cook is therefore confident that "we are entering a period of one or two decades of marvelous invention and creativity that will change the financial services universe."

In chapter 8, **Rosalind Fisher**, executive vice president of VisaNet Services, sees an important role for Visa and its member banks in the electronic payments system. Visa's stored-value card, "Visa Cash," had a successful trial at the 1996 summer Olympic Games in Atlanta and is undergoing other trials around the world. Visa is also working with its members to develop on-line electronic payments. Fisher is confident in the future of the new payments system but recognizes "that premature government regulation—or the failure to modify existing regulations to accommodate evolving technologies—could chill or halt the delivery of new financial products to consumers."

In chapter 9, Representative **Michael N. Castle** (R-DE), chairman of the House Subcommittee on Domestic and International Monetary Policy, summarizes the results of four hearings on "The Future of Money," held during 1995–96. He concludes that the best way to avoid overregulation is for private industry to begin devising "standards . . . for interoperability, privacy, security, financial responsibility, and especially consumer rights." If self-regulation is successful, notes Castle, the full promise of the new electronic payments technology will be realized.

The unanswered question is whether regulators will leave the cybermarket and its evolving electronic payments system alone. In chapter 10, **R. Alton Gilbert**, an economist with the Federal Reserve Bank of St. Louis, contends that the answer hinges on how regulators view the safety and soundness of the emerging electronic payments system. The issue he specifically addresses is whether "nonbank firms whose liabilities are used or will be used for making payments" should be treated as banks and subject to the same supervision and regulation. His interpretation of banking history tells him that market competition and self-regulation are important, but they are not sufficient to prevent crises in the payments system. What is needed is "a central authority for preserving stability of a payments system." Thus, he concludes "that all firms that offer liabilities used by the public for making payments should be required to obtain bank charters . . . be supervised and regulated as banks, and have access to the discount window to help them deal with occasional liquidity problems."

On the question of taxation, **Richard Rahn**, president of Novecon, argues in chapter 11 that the new monetary universe offers an opportunity to adopt a low-rate consumption tax that will stimulate economic growth. If that opportunity is missed, warns Rahn, the elecronic payments system will be used to evade the onerous burden of the present tax system. In a world of anonymous e-money, which can be transferred around the globe at the speed of light, governments everywhere will have to consider Rahn's case for tax reform, since "the more the government tries to tax, regulate, control, and confiscate, the greater the incentive for business and investors to leave." The danger is that if the current tax system is retained, government will become even more intrusive as it tries to stop tax evasion. As Rahn notes, "In the age of the cyberpayment, we cannot both keep the present income tax system and enforce it, and at the same time keep our liberty and privacy."

David Chaum, founder and managing director of DigiCash, presents a way to build an electronic payments system in chapter 12 that will satisfy consumers' demand for privacy while protecting society. He wants to avoid a system of "data fascism," in which every electronic transaction is traceable, but he also thinks that perfect anonymity is not desirable. Paper currency has the merit of allowing its users to remain anonymous, but the costs of using it are high relative to those of an electronic payments system. Chaum's research on blind-signature technology (i.e., the use of encryption to generate secure digital signatures) shows that e-cash can come very close to having the attributes of paper currency without the costs. Moreover, that technology allows users of e-cash to "retroactively and irrefutably reveal the recipient of the funds." Thus, crimes associated with the use of paper currency—such as extortion, bribery, and tax evasion—"are no more likely than they are with checks today." Chaum's goal is to create "a payments system that can be widely adopted and that will stimulate economic growth. . . . and act as a springboard for increasing individual freedom." He believes that goal is achievable once "consumers realize that the use of electronic payments media does not have to compromise their privacy, but in fact can empower them to protect their own interests."

Monetary Policy in the Information Age

The papers in Part III deal with the question of how e-money will affect the conduct of monetary policy. In particular, how will the Federal Reserve's ability to control money and the price level be affected by the transition to an electronic payments system?

In chapter 13, **George Selgin**, a monetary economist at the University of Georgia, argues against the conventional wisdom that financial innovation means the Federal Reserve needs more discretion.

Instead, he contends that innovations such as e-money will provide individuals with more monetary freedom and make them less dependent on the central bank. With less to do, the Fed will not need as much discretionary power to conduct monetary policy. If e-money were to completely crowd out paper currency, the Fed would no longer have to be concerned about variations in the ratio of currency to deposits. Monetary policy then could be more easily directed to controlling the monetary base, argues Selgin. Thus, he considers e-money a friend of monetarists, who have long advocated rules in place of discretion.

Bert Ely, president of Ely & Company, argues in chapter 14 that e-money is unlikely to crowd out paper money because people do not trust the new payments technology. He also argues that e-money will not affect monetary policy. The latter conclusion rests on Ely's assumption that the Federal Reserve is passive in today's financial environment and merely supplies whatever currency and reserves the public and the banking system demand. According to Ely, the only effect e-money will have is to reduce the Fed's profit (seignorage) from issuing currency, insofar as e-money is substituted for central bank money.

In chapter 15, **Jerry Jordan**, president of the Federal Reserve Bank of Cleveland, and **Edward Stevens**, an economist at the bank, expect e-money to crowd out government fiat money and predict that financial innovation is likely to reduce the demand for bank reserves to near zero. Those changes, however, need not reduce the Fed's control over the money supply, according to Jordan and Stevens. That is because "the reliability of monetary policy depends not so much on the amount [of central bank] money demanded as on the predictability of that amount." In their view, "It is much too soon to say whether the predictability . . . will be reduced in any significant way." Moreover, they argue that as long as central bank liabilities are used to settle final payments of taxes and other obligations, the Federal Reserve will continue to "determine the price level."

A more fundamental question, which Jordan and Stevens only touch on, is whether a new monetary standard will emerge as people shift to e-money—that is, will people be willing to hold privately supplied e-money if it is not convertible into central bank money? Moreover, will such a monetary regime be stable? If the answer to both questions is yes, then government fiat monies and central banks may become relics of the 20th century.

In chapter 16, **William Niskanen**, chairman of the Cato Institute, comments on the preceding three chapters. He doubts whether e-money will significantly reduce the public's demand for currency, so he does not expect e-money to have any significant effect on the ratio of currency to deposits or the money multiplier. He favors a monetary rule, but prefers a feedback rule that would target "the nominal level of domestic final sales" to a strict monetary base rule. Niskanen explains that "for a central bank that uses such a recursive, error-correcting monetary policy, a reduction of the variance of the money multiplier is not very important." In sum, he discounts the effect e-money will have on monetary policy and contends that "the regulatory implications of e-money seem more interesting and more important."

The Future of Banking

The information age promises to create an electronic monetary system and expand monetary freedom. How far that freedom reaches and how it may affect the future of banking is the subject of Part IV.

In chapter 17, **Sholom Rosen**, vice president and head of emerging technology at Citibank, describes the progress Citibank has made in developing a secure electronic monetary system and the implications of that system for the future. He states that the new payments technology will allow "EMS notes" to "be created on demand in any currency." Moreover, the electronic monetary system will provide both security and privacy, because it "guarantees the traceability of every note without knowing the identity of the customer." Finally, the EMS—using so-called Trusted Agent technology—will provide protection for both buyers and sellers as they transact over the Internet, ensuring that goods are delivered and payments received. The implication of the new system, writes Rosen, is that "for the first time . . . truly open spontaneous electronic commerce" will be possible.

In chapter 18, **Catherine England**, an economist with the Graduate Business Institute at George Mason University, provides a useful overview of the nature of money and asks how e-money may affect the Fed's position as the sole supplier of currency. She argues that market forces are on the side of private suppliers of e-cash and that those forces will make a system of private competing currencies

9

inherently stable. In the future, she predicts, "What is 'money' will be determined by what buyers and sellers accept and use as money rather than by government definitions." The disappearance of central banking, notes England, will not be a disaster because, as F. A. Hayek (1989: 103) wrote, "The history of government management of money has, except for a few short happy periods, been one of incessant fraud and deception."[1] In particular, "a study of about 30 currencies shows that there has not been a single case of a currency freely manipulated by its government or central bank since 1700 which enjoyed price stability for at least 30 years running" (Bernholz 1990: 104).[2] That dismal record is why it is so important to consider alternatives to government fiat money.

In the final chapter, **F. X. Browne** and **David Cronin**, economists at the Central Bank of Ireland, reason that in the long run a system of laissez-faire banking could evolve as e-money and the model of share banking are widely accepted. They predict that electronic payments and financial innovations could allow individuals to hold all their assets in highly liquid and divisible mutual-fund shares that reflect current market values and, consequently, would represent economically viable exchange media. The resultant "accounting system of exchange" would eliminate the problem of monetary disequilibrium, which is associated with the present par-value "monetary system of exchange." The inherent stability of this private alternative to government fiat money, Browne and Cronin argue, would end the need for banking regulation. Finally, they point out that, while nonbank providers of e-money will compete with banks, banks will probably continue to have a comparative advantage in managing risk in the new monetary universe.

Conclusion

Several policy implications flow from the papers in this volume:

- Low-cost on-line banking and financial innovations will create greater opportunities to escape inefficient domestic financial regulations by moving banking activities offshore, which may

---

[1] In *Choice in Currency*, Hayek (1976: 16) wrote, "What is so dangerous and ought to be done away with is not governments' right to issue money but the *exclusive* right to do so and their power to force people to use it and to accept it a particular price."

[2] Bernholz is referring to the study by Michael Parkin and Robin Bade (1978).

create pressure to remove inefficient regulations at home (chapter 2).

- A secure electronic monetary system will expand financial markets and increase liquidity (trust). As markets expand, the domain of actuarial trust will grow, thereby reducing the problem of moral hazard associated with the guaranteed domain of trust (chapter 3).
- As the information revolution progresses and e-money becomes more widely accepted, there could be added pressure for tax reform, especially for a low-rate consumption tax. Global financial markets will exert even more influence on policymakers to pursue sound policy choices or face massive capital outflows (chapter 11).
- As e-cash crowds out Federal Reserve notes, the Federal Reserve's case for discretion will weaken while the case for monetary rules will strengthen. The adoption of a rules-based monetary regime would reduce institutional uncertainty and provide a more stable monetary unit (chapter 13).
- Finally, in the long run, the electronic payments system may evolve into a system of laissez-faire banking with competing private currencies based on the model of mutual-fund or share banking (chapters 18–19).

In the new monetary universe, people will benefit from more information and more freedom. The danger is that government may try to stifle that information and freedom by overregulation. The challenge is to develop an institutional infrastructure that provides transparent rules for the electronic payments system, safeguards the value of money, and protects individual freedom. There will then be better money and greater wealth as a result of the information revolution. The papers in this volume help lay the intellectual groundwork to meet that challenge.

References

Bernholz, P. (1990) "The Importance of Reorganizing Money, Credit, and Banking When Decentralizing Economic Decisionmaking." In J.A. Dorn and Wang Xi (eds.) *Economic Reform in China: Problems and Prospects*: 93–123. Chicago: University of Chicago Press.
Jordan, J.L. (1995/96) "Governments and Money." *Cato Journal* 15 (2–3) (Fall/Winter): 167–77.

Hayek, F.A. (1976) *Choice in Currency: A Way to Stop Inflation.* Occasional Paper 48. London: Institute of Economic Affairs.

Hayek, F.A. (1989) *The Fatal Conceit: The Errors of Socialism.* Vol. 1 of *The Collected Works of F.A. Hayek.* Edited by W. W. Bartley III. Chicago: University of Chicago Press.

Kelley, E.W. Jr. (1996) Speech given at the Digital Commerce Conference. Washington, D.C., 6 May.

Parkin, M., and Bade, R. (1978) "Central Bank Laws and Monetary Policy: A Preliminary Investigation." In M.A. Porter (ed.) *The Australian Monetary System in the 1970s*: 24–39. Melbourne: Monash University.

PART I

ELECTRONIC COMMERCE
AND MONETARY EVOLUTION

2

THE TECHNOLOGY REVOLUTION AND MONETARY EVOLUTION

Lawrence H. White

When hearing or reading excited discussions of "the new payment technologies" and "digital money" it is well to maintain some historical perspective. What exactly is new, and what difference will it make? Is the coming change in the payments system revolutionary, or better understood as evolutionary? Will changes in the way money is paid from one party to another bring about changes in the character of money itself?

Monetary Evolution, Not Revolution

Digital money—spendable balances represented solely by digits on a bank's balance sheet—is not new. Banking historians have found that merchants in Genoa, Italy, were making payments by transferring bank account balances back in 1200 AD. It doesn't really matter whether the digits on the bank's balance sheet are displayed in ink or in pixels.

What has been changing over the centuries is the usual method of authorizing the transfer of balances from one account to another. In 1200, when Alice wanted to pay Bob by deposit transfer, one or both of them would have to meet in person with a banker to authorize the transfer orally. Paper checks—authorization by written order—came along later, first appearing in the 1300s and becoming common in the 1600s. Remote, paperless, and instantaneously executed authorization of funds transfer, in the form of "wiring" money from one account to another, has been around at the wholesale level since the mid-1900s, following the introduction of the electric

---

Lawrence H. White is Associate Professor of Economics at the University of Georgia.

telegraph. Wire transfer today accounts for the vast majority—more than six-sevenths—of the dollar volume of payments in the United States. (Cash is the most common method by number of transactions per day, but the estimated average value of a cash transaction is tiny, $10, compared to that of a wire transfer, $4 million.) What is called electronic funds transfer or EFT, wherein an individual accesses the payment system by means of a debit card reader or a personal computer, basically brings the wiring of money down to the level of the retail transaction.

What makes EFT significant is that it considerably lowers the cost of wiring money. The most obvious result to be expected is a reduction in the frequency of check-writing. Debit cards are now proliferating widely, bill-paying by personal computer is finally catching on, and deposit transfer via the Internet appears to be coming soon. People who today receive glossy catalogs, order merchandise by telephone, and pay by reading a credit card number to an operator, may in a few years find it more convenient to shop on-line by personal computer, and pay on-line by clicking an on-screen "buy" button to authorize a deposit transfer to the seller's account. (On-line payment by credit card is already available at many commercial Web sites today.) But these are evolutionary rather than revolutionary changes, and superficial rather than profound. What happens behind the scenes—deposit transfer—remains the same.

The Transition to Digital Currency

A second form of digital money—an alternative to the deposit-transfer method of payment—has recently appeared on the horizon. Developments in cryptography are said to be bringing us what we can call "digital currency." The currency balance information, an encoded string of digits, can be carried on a "smart" plastic card with an implanted microchip, or kept on a computer hard drive. Like a traveler's check, a digital currency balance is a floating claim on a bank or other financial institution that is not linked to any particular account. One cardholder can make a payment to another *without bank involvement*, by placing both cards in a "digital wallet" that writes down the card balance on one card and writes up the balance on the other by the same amount. Desktop electronic currency transfers can similarly be made by electronic mail. A card's digital currency balance can be "topped up" by placing it in an

ATM (a PC's balance by getting on-line with the bank) and down-loading funds from one's account. Like paper currency and coins (which we can conveniently call "analog currency"), digital currency balances are circulating bearer media. If personal information is omitted from the balance transfer information (unlike current prac-tice in debit- and credit-card transactions), the bearer can remain anonymous. An issuing bank need only know the total of its out-standing currency liabilities, not who holds them at any moment.

First Union, NationsBank, and other banks have already begun issuing a prototype "digital currency" in the form of prepaid "cash cards" whose balances can be spent down. (Residual balances can be redeemed or applied to the purchase of a new card.) As I under-stand the technology, however, the balances Alice pays to Bob cannot be added to Bob's card. They cannot be respent without bank involvement, but must be deposited by Bob, and thereby (directly or indirectly via the clearing system) presented to the issuing bank for verification and addition to Bob's deposit balances. Balances on prepaid cards (and on PC's and smart cards that share this feature) are consequently more like digital cashier's checks than like circulat-ing currency.

What is new in true digital currency is not the creation of anony-mous bearer claims against private banks. Private bank notes, paper-borne bearer claims issued by banks in round denominations, have been the predominant form of currency throughout history when and where governments do not seize a monopoly of paper currency issue. They continue to form the common currency today in Scotland, Northern Ireland, and Hong Kong, where local commercial banks have never completely lost their right of issue.

The incentive for banks to offer digital currency is clear: float. If digital currency balances pay zero interest, as analog currency traditionally has, the bank receives an interest-free loan from custom-ers holding its currency balances. I imagine that personal computers and even smart cards could be programmed to pay interest on digital currency balances, augmenting the unspent balance each day by a prespecified percentage. If such programming can be developed and cheaply copied to PCs and smart cards, competition will force the banks that issue digital currency to pay interest on it, presumably at a rate similar to what they pay on bank deposits, leaving the banks with a spread just sufficient to cover the costs of issuing digital currency. Interest on digital currency would make small-denomination currency interest-bearing for the first time in history. Such a development, combined with anonymity, would enhance the prospects for the public's turning away from government-issued notes and coins. The only remaining sellers who would continue to accept analog currency would be those whose transaction volume is too small to justify an investment in the hardware necessary to receive digital currency payments or electronic deposit transfers. As the hardware becomes cheaper and card use more common, the set of such sellers will increasingly shrink. Once it falls below critical mass, and consumers no longer routinely carry cash, the use of analog currency could practically disappear.

Ending Government's Monopoly of Currency

Suppose that analog currency does disappear from common circulation. Does this usher in a world without money, as some writers have suggested? No. Rather, it "merely" undoes the current government monopoly of currency. It returns us to a world where the commonly seen money is privately issued, as it was in sophisticated economies 150 years ago where gold coin was seldom seen outside bank vaults despite being the ultimate money of redemption for deposits and bank notes. Payments continue to be money payments, transfers of deposits and currency. Bank-issued monies continue to be claims to an ultimate or "base" money. In the current U.S. monetary system base money comes in two forms: Federal Reserve Notes and commercial bank clearing deposits on the books of the Fed. Eliminating the first (by the public voluntarily swapping its holdings with banks in exchange for bank-issued money) would not eliminate the second. In fact the total stock of base money need not change, as banks would swap the Federal Reserve Notes turned in by the public for Fed deposit claims (still indispensable for settling net flows of funds between banks). Bank deposits at the Fed would constitute the entire stock of base money.

The transition from analog to digital currency therefore does not change the monetary standard: the base money remains a fiat money, and bank-issued money remains a redeemable claim to fiat money. It is possible that the disappearance of Federal Reserve notes will make the unanchored nature of the fiat dollar standard more obvious to the public, but a change in the standard will not automatically follow. A switch to some kind of commodity standard will require a public debate and deliberate public decision.

The Question of Monetary Control

Do electronic funds transfer and the private issue of digital currency undermine the central bank's ability to control the total quantity of money in the economy? No. (In fact, as my colleague George Selgin argues, it may even make the Fed's job easier.) Electronic funds transfer merely moves money from one holder to another; it does not itself change the aggregate quantity. The quantity of transaction balances *or digital currency* a bank can prudently create is naturally limited by the bank's contractual obligation (without which the public would not accept bank-issued money to begin with) to convert its liabilities on demand into scarce reserve money (analog currency or its account balance at the clearinghouse). Thus even with banks "creating their own money" the Fed has undiminished control over the aggregate quantity of money (whether measured as M1, M2, or whatever) via its undiminished control over the quantity of base money. If the Fed mistakenly thought that digital currency undermined its monetary control, it could of course impose the same reserve requirements against outstanding digital currency liabilities that it now imposes against deposit balances.

The Potential for Offshore Banking

So what real difference will digital currency and desktop EFT make? What strikes me as the most exciting potential development to come from the new payment technologies is that, as they lower the cost of wiring money from $20 to 2 cents or less per transaction, they give ordinary small savers affordable access to offshore banking. With direct deposit of paychecks, and with analog currency available at ATMs whenever we want it, many of us no longer need to visit our bank in person. Why not keep your account with a reputable bank (perhaps a branch of a major Swiss bank) in the Bahamas or Cayman Islands? Such an account is perfectly legal for U.S. citizens (though the offshore branch of a U.S. bank is prohibited from directly doing business with American citizens or firms). Offshore banks pay higher interest on deposits (and charge lower interest on loans) than domestic banks because they are free from the taxes on deposit balances that the U.S. government levies in the

19

form of reserve requirements, deposit "insurance premiums," and taxes on bank earnings. Big-money players have enjoyed the advantages of offshore banking for years. Small firms and individuals do not find it worth accessing the offshore banking market today because the current expense of wiring money back and forth more than consumes the extra interest earned on small sums of money. Cheap desktop electronic funds transfer will make offshore banking a smart move for small savers. If an offshore bank were linked into an onshore clearinghouse (and an onshore ATM network for providing analog currency, as long as analog currency survives), it could also attract transaction account customers. Individuals concerned about privacy might find an offshore foreign bank attractive for its lesser propensity to surrender its records to domestic authorities.

When commercial on-line networks and Internet sites begin offering offshore banking services, with zero or very small fees for transferring funds, an exodus of retail banking business will begin from the regulated onshore sector to the untaxed and unregulated offshore sector. The depositors left behind will be those traditionalists who like to do their banking business in person (many households are not yet on-line; and some people still refuse to use ATMs), and those who think that FDIC insurance is worth its price—despite the fact that uninsured offshore bank deposits have proven safe throughout the postwar era.

3

ELECTRONIC LIQUIDITY AND DOMAINS OF TRUST

William Melton

The very term electronic money (e-money) carries with it so much hype, so many misconceptions, so many private agendas, that thoughtful discussion becomes difficult. Therefore, let me avoid that emotion-laden word and instead focus on electronic liquidity. In the consumer world, all that matters is liquidity—namely, whether the receiver will readily accept the marker presented as a valid medium of exchange. The source of that liquidity, whether from a line of credit, a bank deposit, or a gift certificate, is not important. What is important is that liquidity be reliable and convenient. Consumers want to know: Is this transaction going to "bounce," come undone, or unravel? What is the nuisance factor? How many forms do I have to fill out? And how long do I have to wait to complete the transaction?

Liquidity and Trust

Liquidity has a strong psychological variable, indeed its principal element is trust. In the technical world of cryptography, we talk about domains of trust. Let me suggest that liquidity can only be produced from a domain of trust. And those domains can be one of at least two types: a domain of actuarial trust or a domain of guaranteed trust.

A Domain of Actuarial Trust

Life insurance companies can trust they will have a certain investment horizon for your policy, based on actuarial tables. The life

---

William Melton is Chief Executive Officer of CyberCash, Inc.

insurance company does not get your pastor, your mother, or your banker to guarantee you will live to a certain age. The insurance company, sadly to say, is not even very concerned what age you live to, except as it may affect their actuarial averages.

A major grocery chain is willing to accept checks from strangers because the actuarial experience of grocers has shown that less than one half of 1 percent of those checks will go bad.

Obviously life insurance companies and grocery stores will try to tweak the odds: with life insurance companies accepting only nonsmokers or grocery stores rejecting checks with low check numbers. But fundamentally, the trust comes from actuarial dynamics, not from some external guarantor.

A Domain of Guaranteed Trust

The second type of trust domain is one that we are more familiar with: the domain of guaranteed trust. In this type of domain, the government, the bank, or some other strong guarantor says, "Trust me, I guarantee it." Behind any guarantor there may be another guarantor, such as behind your bank stands the Federal Deposit Insurance Corporation, and behind the FDIC is the perceived strength of the government. Thus, these guaranteed trust domains quickly become very hierarchical.

Frequently, there is a mixing of actuarial and guaranteed trust domains. For example, though you as employer may not personally know all of your 500 employees, you believe you have followed good hiring practices and therefore you can say to your bank: "Please extend to my employees liquidity for travel expenses, and I will make good if anyone fails to pay." You have made the actuarial assessment of trust internally, then converted that into a guaranteed trust in dealing with the bank. The bank does not have a clue about your employees; it is looking to your guarantee for its trust.

The distinction between liquidity based on actuarial analysis and on a guarantor relation, although subtle, has substantial social, political, and economic implications. The actuarial domain of trust is frequently found in a market economy, while the guaranteed domain of trust is more at home in hierarchical environments. Modern financial markets spring from the sharing of risk and are actuarial by nature. Even the largest guarantors (governments) are subject to the statistical evaluations of those markets or actuarial domains. As a national and international economy, the United States is moving, and must move, toward actuarial domains of trust.

Electronic Liquidity

We can now apply the concepts of actuarial and guaranteed trust domains to specifically electronic liquidity. I will suggest that electronic liquidity can be substantially and safely increased without inflationary impact. This increase of electronic liquidity with a corresponding increase in goods and services will happen inevitably by trial and error driven by entrepreneurial effort. But to understand this increase of both electronic liquidity and the corresponding increase in goods and service, it is worthwhile to have a better understanding of both actuarial and guaranteed trust domains, and the evolution of those domains.

The Visa and MasterCard systems can serve as an example. In the early days Visa and MasterCard established a wonderfully creative system of cross guarantees and then enabled that guarantee system with cutting-edge telecom technology. As a consumer your local banker guaranteed liquidity for you. The merchant's banker guaranteed liquidity for him. Each of you stayed inside your own preexisting domain of trust. The cutting edge telecom systems linked these two domains of trust with wires, protocols, and operating procedures.

While each local bank acted as a strong guarantor, total system risks were handled actuarially by assessments to the participating banks. Again, note the novel mixing of guaranteed trust systems (locally) with actuarial trust systems (systemwide), enabled by new telecom technologies.

Obviously no system stands still. It evolves and certainly the Visa and MasterCard systems have evolved. As telecom systems became ever more efficient, the merchant bank's "value add" became less (measured as a percentage of the total transaction cost). Thus, the acquirer (or merchant's) bank provided an ever declining relative value. Transaction approval costs (a merchant bank's function) have dropped from perhaps 30 cents in the early 1980s to roughly 3 cents now. The merchants' banks "value add" became ever more technical, commoditized, and out-sourced. Thus, there has been huge consolidation on the merchant bank side of the transaction. Trust (i.e., liquidity) on the merchant side of the transaction now comes from

23

technical prowess rather than from maintaining a personal banking relationship with the merchants.

Today a larger share of the revenue and profits goes to the consumers' end of the transaction. This is where the liquidity is extended, or where the liquidity is created. Here the issuing banks continue to shine and continue to make large profits. But even here there has been rapid and dramatic movement toward an actuarial trust domain. Aggressive banks now routinely issue liquidity to customers whom they have never seen, on a nationwide basis. State boundaries are thin veils to be nodded at in passing. With the help of massive data bases, sophisticated scoring techniques, and carefully delineated actuarial domains, banks issue billions of dollars of liquidity based solely on actuarial trust.

But a funny thing has happened on the way to this great outpouring of liquidity. The cost of distribution (that is, the cost of getting the liquidity to the consumer) is more expensive than evaluating and granting the credit or liquidity. By today's economics, it might cost $50 to $70, including advertising and mailings, to acquire a new bank liquidity customer. At the same time, using advanced actuarial techniques it might cost less that $10 to evaluate and complete the granting of the credit or liquidity.

Thus, distribution and marketing costs have become the tall pole in the tent on the road to providing consumer liquidity. Crudely explained, if you were running a mint, and the cost of the precious metals or the cost of printing were no longer significant, but rather the cost of distributing your money was now 90 percent of your budget, you would obviously focus on those costs. Moreover, if a competitive mint had zero costs of distribution, its money may well, in a competitive market, gain market share. To a large extent this is the situation in the consumer liquidity granting environment today.

To solve the problem of high distribution costs, aggressive players have begun to rely on existing natural groupings (e.g., United Airlines' Visa Card). These groupings already support distribution infrastructure and costs for their own pre-existing purposes. In the banking world these are known as "affinity" or "co-branding" efforts.

As we move to the newer and ever evolving world of the Internet, the relative distribution and mind-share acquisition costs become even more extreme. The need to use affinity groups, subgroups, special interest groups, and specific purpose groups, in an effort to rise above the white noise of nearly infinite information flow, becomes quickly apparent and urgent.

Each subgroup used as a distribution channel will ask for some benefit for their assistance in the distribution of liquidity, the mint product. The market will become ever more differentiated with rewards for specific skills such as "just distribution," or "distribution and credit guarantee," or just "credit guarantee."

In a traditional physical world such complexity and convoluted relations would soon become too costly to manage. However with modern computers and telecommunications links, it is now possible to profitably use the Sierra Club as an actuarial grouping and distribution partner. As we move further into the world of the Internet and further down the road of electronic liquidity, we will economically be able to manage ever greater differentiation and even finer granularity.

There will be coupons, interactive game prizes, rewards for the best song or best poem. There will be corporate petty cash boxes, school fund-raising drives, and a myriad of other closed-end or limited-use liquidity systems. These limited-use liquidity systems will meld with and help distribute more traditional liquidity instruments from more traditional players.

In an economic environment so complex, and probably highly leveraged, breakage in any one area, unless contained, could be dangerous for the whole system. Therefore, local reserves managed by the market "experts," whether those be traditional bankers or the stock market, will be used as firewalls to contain "actuarial mistakes" within small local pockets.

Actuarial systems work well only when there can be reliable tracking and statistical feedback continually updating the actuarial model. Such tracking raises the specter of personal identity tracking and potential losses of personal privacy. Without going into the details, suffice it to say that maintaining most any degree of privacy is *not* contradictory to adequate statistical feedback. In any transaction there is the identity of the guarantor, the identity of the asset or account holder, the identity of the liquidity or credit issuer, and the identity of the shopper or conveyer. Any or all of these various identities can be exchanged, blinded, or proxied to provide whatever level of privacy is appropriate for that type of transaction. Yet, because the actuarial system is interested in the epidemiological behavior of the actuarial group as a whole, rather than individual behavior, the benefits of an actuarial domain of trust can be preserved while maintaining full privacy.

As actuarial trust domains become more differentiated, filling many niches that heretofore could not be envisioned, the total system will still be able to manage these interacting complex identity sets in an efficient manner. Digital certificates, digital signatures, private certificate authorities, and increasingly capable actuarial evaluation and scoring systems will easily manage complexity at lower costs than is possible today.

The Challenge of the Marketplace

If chains of trust are the primary ingredient of liquidity, then the technology of digital signatures and digital certificates are the technological breakthroughs that allow maintenance of ever more subtle, more complex, and yet still reliable, chains and domains of trust. The economic impact is to provide greater liquidity. Yet, this additional liquidity is provided under the tight feedback loops of the market and is, on the whole, noninflationary.

The liquidity (in all of its various forms) provided by these evolving systems will stimulate sales, not only of existing goods and services, but more importantly this more efficient electronic liquidity will stimulate production of new goods and services, services that cannot today be economically provided.

In traditional economics we assumed, for simplicity of discussion, that there was a finite amount of goods and services available in the marketplace. I take issue with this mechanistic assumption of finite market limits. Is there a limit to the number of songs that can be produced or enjoyed? Are the number of ideas that can be thought finite? Are the number of computer programs to be written finite? Are ideas about efficiency itself finite? I would argue, no, there is an infinite progression, and therefore potentially an infinite supply of goods and services.

The challenge of the marketplace and the newer forms of electronic liquidity is to continually lower transactions costs, continually increase convenience, and thereby enable new markets heretofore not possible. With strong actuarial feedback, it is also the job of the market to match the supply of these new forms of liquidity with the equivalent supply of goods and services coming from both old and new markets.

I am extremely optimistic about the enabling power of increasing efficiency and convenience in payment systems and in the granting of liquidity. I am doubly optimistic about the power of the marketplace that is being born on the Internet, a marketplace where geography has largely evaporated and time is measured in baud rates. These combined efficiencies, I believe, can bring society a new age of plenty and opportunity. We live in exciting times.

4

THE INTERNET AND THE END OF MONETARY SOVEREIGNTY

Bill Frezza

Almost 40 years ago Ayn Rand, in her novel *Atlas Shrugged*, posed the question: "What would happen if the men of the mind—the producers and creators of wealth—went on strike?" Her allegory about the coordinated withdrawal of the industrialists and the collapse of civilization served as a dramatic backdrop for the elucidation of her moral philosophy. That philosophy, rooted in laissez-faire capitalism, posed two questions relevant to the issue of monetary sovereignty: What creates the value of money? And who stands sovereign in a struggle between individuals who use their productive powers to create wealth and governments who wield coercive force to redistribute it?

While a generation of free-market thinkers were deeply influenced by her ideas, Rand and her followers were unable to generate a practical political program. The fact that the value of money rests not on the power to compel but on the ability to produce remains a mystery not only to the public but to many economists. History also tells us that sovereignty in economic affairs has never been based on a web of consensual agreements. Instead, it invariably rests on the power to confiscate, imprison, and coerce. If there is any doubt on this point, even as applied to the world's most civilized democracies, imagine how long the IRS would stay in business if it lost this power.

The romantic notion of a conspiracy of the productive rebelling against these facts of life makes for a great novel but is hopelessly

Bill Frezza is President of Wireless Computing Associates, Inc. He is also the cofounder of the on-line forum Digital Liberty (http://www.digitaliberty.org).

impractical as a blueprint to reverse the growth of the leviathan state. What Rand could not foresee, and the challenge that confronts us now, is that technology would create a new world in which the fundamental facts of life have indeed changed. That world is called cyberspace and its growing backbone is the Internet. The Internet will not merely make our existing forms of commerce more efficient, but will support the emergence of self-organizing, supranational communities whose economic intercourse can be based on exactly the principles Rand espoused.

The World of Cyberspace

It will never be possible to transport wheat or steel across a wire, and real economies will always continue to produce and consume wheat and steel. But any product of the human mind can be communicated as a stream of digital bits. And it is exactly this sector of our economy—the product of our minds—that is growing the fastest. It is in the information industries, broadly defined, that the majority of the world's new wealth is being created, the wealth upon which the value of money will someday be based.

We know that wealth can be exchanged electronically, both in the form of new monetary instruments and, equally important, in the actual content of the products and services that will be delivered over the Internet. It is possible, then, that a referent to external physical commodities or existing fiat currencies may not always be necessary to establish the value of money within cyberspace. While a self-supporting cyberspace currency may be impractical today, the possibility of achieving independence from external referents will certainly increase as the portion of the world's wealth that exists in cyberspace grows. After all, in a few generations a significant fraction of the world's economy might well have no material existence whatsoever. While this may sound bizarre, it is no more radical an idea than imagining, back at the turn of this century, that our nation could feed 250 million people with only a small proportion of the population employed as farmers, or that we could sustain an advanced standard of living with a shrinking minority of our citizens engaged in manufacturing.

The pressing question, then, is how might a political economy based on exchanging intangibles in cyberspace differ from a political economy based on exchanging wheat or steel in the real world?

First and foremost, privacy in cyberspace will not be an abstract political right based on the vagaries of geography, government policy, or cultural norms. In the future, electronic privacy will be an absolute algorithmic certainty. The science of cryptology, long an exclusive province of government security agencies, has taken root in the private sector. While governments may retard the promulgation of strong encryption, they can at best forestall the inevitable. The failure and irrelevancy of the Clinton administration's Clipper Chip key escrow initiative is a testament to the futility of trying to control this technology. The day will inevitably come when the amount of effort required to breach the shield of privacy provided by low-cost, widely available encryption will exceed the value of such an attack by so many orders of magnitude that it will not be economically feasible to base public policy on such invasions. Governments of the world will have to live with the fact that they will be impotent to pry into many of their citizens' economic affairs.

Second, cyberspace differs from our everyday world in that coercive force cannot be projected across a network. It is not possible, within the confines of the Internet itself, to compel anyone to do anything. This is a discomfiting revelation to most legislators, who like to pretend that their power rests on the consent of the governed rather than the barrel of a gun. Sooner or later, however, any assertion of sovereignty over actions that take place entirely within cyberspace—whether it is the transmission of banned materials, the regulation and taxation of consensual economic transactions, or even the creation of money—must resort to acts of physical coercion or threats thereof.

To do so, however, requires that the target be identified and located. It will always be possible to do this for Fortune 500 companies, whose vast visible assets make them conspicuously vulnerable. Those large entities, therefore, may never be able to fully avail themselves of the new freedoms that will emerge in cyberspace. But it is going to get very difficult to keep track of the growing number of individuals and contingent or part-time knowledge workers who are rapidly learning to ply their trades on the Internet. Sophisticated networking tools guaranteeing anonymity, such as the chains of anonymous reforwarders being set up worldwide, will make unwanted identification and location harder and harder, particularly if the number of people using these tools in the routine course of business grows. And given the globalization of commerce made possible by the Internet, allowing even solitary individuals to transact business around the world, the target of any particular act of coercion is as likely as not to be in a political jurisdiction inaccessible by the aggrieved government agency.

What does that mean in a practical sense? It means that ordinary people will be able to create and exchange wealth outside the prying eyes and grasping hands of sovereign powers. And they will not have to retreat from society to a utopian enclave to do that, or make a full time career out of tax avoidance. In fact, most individuals won't even have to quit their day jobs. All that will be required is a PC, some off-the-shelf software, an Internet account, and a little excess time. Imagine the consequences if a significant fraction of the world's most productive people took a portion of their work output and used it to engage in unrestrained commerce within an economic system inherently immune from government scrutiny. The wealth produced—that is, the underlying products of their creative output upon which the value of money will be based—may never exist in the physical world. And since this wealth may not have to be exchanged with government fiat currency in order to be useful, there may be scant opportunity to seize it. This is going to be treated as a grave threat by most national governments.

The Coming Battle

A battle for cyberspace most certainly lies ahead, and you can expect entrenched bureaucrats to do everything they can to demonize the new technology by associating it with pornographers, child molesters, and drug-money launderers. Judging from the sensational and wildly distorted coverage of the Internet in the popular press, the old media appear to be fully cooperating in this propaganda campaign. But can this approach be sustained as the Internet achieves mass-market penetration? Can the behavior of millions of people really be controlled once unequivocally verifiable, mathematically unforgeable, and unconditionally untraceable digital cash appears in widespread circulation? Who will be able to resist when, with the click of a mouse, it will be so easy to disappear? Imagine what would happen if the productive efforts of millions were invisible to the IRS, gone from the GNP statistics, blind to the balance of trade, and immune to social or industrial policy mandates.

A New Liberty

Perhaps, in cyberspace, a new liberty lies ahead, one in which Rand's strict Objectivism can finally be reconciled with libertarianism, a political movement whose anarchist elements Rand so much despised. Perhaps, for the first time, sovereign individuals will have the tools to construct a practical realization of laissez-faire capitalism without having to resort to a problematic social contract with an all-powerful state to create the conditions necessary to sustain a stable political economy. At the root of this system will be new monetary institutions that must inherently rest on the consent of the participants.

Cyberspace, which promises to shield individuals from the ravages of coercive force and allow them to conduct their affairs in secure anonymity, will bring forth a burst of creative human genius not seen since the last time a new world was discovered. If *Atlas Shrugged* were written today, imagine how it might turn out.

5

THE TECHNOLOGICAL REALITIES OF INTERNET COMMERCE

Lawrence Gasman

There is a story from the 1840s, a period when the electric telegraph was creating almost as much excitement as the World Wide Web does at present. In the story, a farmer responds to all the fuss over the new technology with some skepticism and he places a wager. He bets that his horse can deliver a message faster than the telegraph.

The story is probably apocryphal, no more than a joke. But like all good jokes it makes a serious point. The story about the farmer and his horse makes fun of those who have no conception of how the new technology works. Horses seldom travel at the speed of light.

Of course, this story is barely funny any more, because, for most of us, some level of understanding of telegraphic technology is embedded in our general knowledge. However, many of us do not possess similar depth when it comes to the Internet, and there is a tendency to predict the impact of Internet based on notions that are not in tune with its technology.

Within the world of commerce and banking, there are those who see the Internet as no more than a vital new way to reach their customers in a cost-effective manner. Banks in particular have seized on the Internet as one way to solve the problem of the escalating costs of having human tellers spend long amounts of time dealing with smaller depositors. At the other end of the scale there are those who see in the Internet and its World Wide Web a mechanism for banking and commerce entirely free from the dead hand of regulation and central banks. For libertarians this is the dream. For central

---

Lawrence Gasman is Director of Telecommunications and Technology Studies at the Cato Institute.

bankers and the managers of large financial institutions it is the nightmare.

My personal view of the future is closer to the libertarian dream than the bankers' nightmare. I think that the view of the Internet as just being another marketing tool is a gross underestimation of what the Internet will mean to us all within a few years. Viewing the Internet as just another marketing channel is essentially the late 21st century equivalent of the farmer's story with which this paper began.

But, as usually expressed, many current views of what the Internet will mean to us seem to exist in a rarefied environment that largely fails to take into account the technological reality of the Internet. As a result, some of the claims made for the potential of the Internet are overstated. The purpose of this paper is to redress that imbalance, if only by a little.

What Is Special About the Internet?

Today's Internet is a triumph for both human ingenuity and spontaneous order. In some parts it embodies leading-edge technology, such as SONET—a high-speed transmission standard—or Asynchronous Transfer Mode (ATM)—a powerful switching and multiplexing technology. But most users dial up their Internet service provider using 1870s technology—a regular analog telephone line. Many Internet service providers connect up their network nodes using 1970s technology—T1 (1.5 Mbps) and T3 (45 Mbps) digital lines. Even the World Wide Web is an ingenious mix of established Windows technology and hypertext linking. Hypertext has been pushed as a human-machine interface since at least the 1970s.

It is not new technology then that created the excitement about the Internet and the World Wide Web in the commercial and banking worlds. Rather it is a innovative combination of older technologies that appears to create a radical new trading environment. Specifically it is claimed that (1) the Internet ends distance limitations, and (2) the Internet empowers individuals in important new ways to create new commercial and financial entities.

In this paper, I examine these claims against the realities of current and emerging technologies, and I analyze the implications of those technologies for banking and commerce from a market-liberal perspective.

The End of Distance

Classical telephone communications has been distance limited in two senses. First, the further the call, the more it cost. Second, until quite recently, the further the call, the poorer the quality of connection. The quality of long-distance service has improved, so that a call from Toronto to Tokyo can be as clear as a call from New York to Newark, although calls to Third-World countries may still be problematic.

But telephone calls are still charged by distance. Even if you lease a private line, you are charged by how far that private line extends. The Internet is quite different: users pay only for access to the Internet; after that the ride is free. It is just as easy to call up an American Web site from Chicago as it is from London. Indeed the physical location of the server on which the Web Site is located may be unknown to someone visiting the site. It may even be unknown to the person who owns the site.

Those who look on the Internet as no more than a marketing opportunity see distance independence as an opportunity to carry out direct marketing to a self-selected international audience at very little cost. Taking this a little further, bankers see here an opportunity to win an international clientele for their products and services, relatively free from the burdens of regulation. But they would certainly stop short of endorsing the libertarian dream of free banking on the Web.

The libertarian dream is not completely tied to the notion of low-cost access and distance independence. Obviously, we can carry out transactions with foreign banks to our hearts' content over regular telephone lines if we are willing to pay the high transaction costs. But the libertarian vision of the ordinary citizen carrying out his banking transactions on a regular basis with some private banking entity in the Cayman Islands is obviously dependent on transactions costs remaining low.

The assumption is made almost universally that the transactions made on the Internet will never be distance dependent, but this may not be the case. It is true that the costs associated with the packet-switching technology that underpins the Internet are less distanced based than older telephone networks, but a long-distance packet call still travels over a lot more expensive transmission systems and switching equipment than a short-haul call. Thus, the costs of

Internet services are less determined by geography than the old telephone system, but they are not entirely geographically invariant.

It is at least plausible to imagine forces that could come into play that could transform the current situation. Economics may be the most powerful such force. Because users currently only pay for Internet access, it has been claimed that there is a strong incentive to develop and deploy access facilities but considerably less incentive to improve on the long-distance backbone infrastructure that supports the Internet.

Of course, market forces may set access pricing for the Internet and distribute funds in a way that supports both access and backbone facilities. Nevertheless, it seems quite likely that current Internet pricing mechanisms (and certainly the pricing expectations of the cyberspace culture, which tends to see any non-zero pricing as a conspiracy of big business) reflect the Internet's origin as a network supported by the taxpayer and that Internet pricing will have to change significantly in the next few years to reflect new commercial realities.

Will such changes include distance-based pricing? Probably not—at least not immediately. The logic of Internet technology points to continued distance independence. For a start, that is what virtually all Internet users expect. It will be hard to change this business model for the Internet now. Second, the packet-switching technology that underpins the Internet was specifically designed to provide very cost-effective long-distance transport for computer data. Third, in most cases Internet service providers do not have billing systems that could bill by distance.

Nevertheless, the mechanisms for distance-based pricing are beginning to emerge. Already, MCI offers a distance-based pricing option for its frame relay data service. This is intended to provide corporate frame relay users, who need the service for regional rather than national networking, with a price break. But frame relay is a technology that is now widely used by smaller Internet service providers to provide themselves with backbone facilities. So charging by distance is not inconceivable, and that possibility is heightened by the fact that billing systems are a major area of research and development in the telephone industry at the present time. Thus, effective ways for Internet service providers to charge by distance seem certain to emerge.

There may even be some regulatory pressures to bring about distance-based charging on the Internet. Some of the small long-distance carriers are protesting to the FCC about voice traffic being carried on the Internet. They claim that they are being discriminated against, because long-distance telephone companies have to pay special fees mandated by regulators to the local telephone companies that provide their links to the customer, while Internet service providers do not have to pay such fees. Their point—and it is not an unjust one—is that this gives an unfair advantage to the Internet service providers and may ultimately destroy the telephone industry if it loses the voice traffic that accounts for the overwhelming majority of its business.

At this point it seems that the protests against voice on the Internet will be unsuccessful, if only because the chorus is not being joined by the big three long-distance carriers—AT&T, MCI, and Sprint—who see a profitable future in being Internet service providers themselves. But this situation could change and perhaps some day regulators will demand that the Internet service providers behave more like long-distance carriers and charge by distance.

Such a regulatory move could be prompted by lobbying not just from the potential losers in the telephone industry, but also from those in the financial services industry who see in the Internet the threat of consumers moving to offshore banks and, in the long term, the end of central banking. This is not an implausible scenario, for while the Internet may be unregulatable in a global sense, the regulation of domestically based Internet service providers is certainly a possibility.

The Limits to Individual Empowerment

The other claim that is made for the Internet, or more specifically the World Wide Web, is that it offers a powerful new tool for entrepreneurs. The point here is that anyone with the small amount of capital needed to open a CompuServe or America Online account has at his or her command most of the resources to build a Web site, which can be used as the platform for a business entity, perhaps even a cyberspace banking corporation. And while the server space available from the main on-line services is limited, space on other servers is available for modest rates with a rapidly growing community of Web Masters able and willing to serve the needs of entrepreneurs anxious to establish their own Web sites.

However, it is not just the availability of resources that is important here. It is the power of those resources. Business people and hobbyists have been setting up their own computer bulletin board systems for more than a decade, but these have been almost entirely text-based, with poor graphics. Web sites using the standard HTML programming language can easily incorporate sophisticated graphic images. Moreover, HTML's extension, VRML, promises to add virtual reality capabilities to the Web, while Sun's Java language offers multimedia capabilities including the power to incorporate moving images and sound.

There is little doubt that these capabilities will add powerful new marketing capabilities to the Web. But it is not just the presentation qualities of the Web that have attracted so much attention. It is also the fact that visitors to Web sites are self-selected. Web sites are much more like retail stores in that people choose to visit them. Contrast this with advertising or direct marketing where most recipients have no interest in the product being marketed. Adding even more excitement is the fact that even relatively small amounts of investment can produce Web sites visited by thousands of potential customers every week—perhaps every day.

All this has excited the marketing imagination to view the World Wide Web as an important new platform for commercial activity. This, I believe, is a correct assessment. The libertarian imagination has, however, taken the process one step further.

Libertarians frequently claim that the development of the Web is leading us to a brave new world in which small entrepreneurs will rise from nowhere, selling "third wave" products and services on the Internet, receiving electronic money in payment, and acting out of reach of government regulation.

There is some validity to this scenario, but as with the "end of distance" scenario described earlier, it is an exaggeration—perhaps a gross exaggeration—of the facts.

The Web does indeed offer new opportunities for entrepreneurs, and it lowers the barriers to entry in many sectors, but in the end the Web will probably come to be dominated by a relatively small number of marketing and financial services entities, just as other markets do when they mature. These entities may be the giants of today—K-mart and Citicorp, for example—or they may be companies that have yet to be born, the next generation of Microsoft and Netscape.

This type of scenario irritates those in the cyberspace community who are more than a little paranoid about big business. But such worries are somewhat irrational. First, in mature markets dominated by a few firms, it is still quite usual for there to be many successful smaller firms profitably serving the needs of market niches. Second, attacks on big business too often ignore the fact that big business gets that way by providing consumers with what they want and the fact that bigness itself can sometimes be a virtue.

This latter point is particularly important in the context of financial services provided over the Web. The Web may indeed create some opportunities for free banking with Web sites serving as proxies for offshore banks and physical money being replaced by some kind of electronic surrogate. However, it seems unlikely that the migration to cyberspace will alleviate financial entities from the need to back their activities with large amounts of assets.

This factor is enhanced in a world free from banking regulations, such as the one that some libertarians imagine for cyberspace. Who wants to bank with an institution that has neither backing from a large government or its own large resources?

The Price of Freedom

And will banks on the Web really be free from government interference? I have already pointed out that while the Web may be difficult to control, domestic Internet service providers are as easy to regulate as any other long-distance carrier. Similarly, Web sites, though the presence may be felt mainly in cyberspace, are no more than programs residing on computers located within national borders. Disk drives can be smashed just as easily as printing presses but there are more of them—and if you know the feds are coming, it is easier to shift your computer elsewhere.

Marketers and bankers who see new opportunities in electronic commerce as the result of the Web are correct in their analysis—the Web changes the economics of many businesses, although it does not change the laws of economics. They are also correct in thinking that the Web subverts national borders, there will be easy ways to route around most barriers to cross-border transactions.

But it is important for those of us who are of the libertarian persuasion not to think of the Web as a sort of commercial version of the platonic heaven, entirely free from the ravages of government action. Ultimately, it has a physical reality rooted in hardware, software, and human organizations, much like the human organizations we have always known and with the same weaknesses.

Even if some day the Web becomes the main avenue for commerce, its freedom will need to be protected by a system of laws made and continually supported by wise men and women. If this analysis is correct, then the price of free commerce and free banking on the Net will be much the same as for freedom itself—namely, eternal vigilance.

FINANCIAL INNOVATION, REGULATION, AND TAXATION

6

FOSTERING FINANCIAL INNOVATION: THE ROLE OF GOVERNMENT

Alan Greenspan

You have heard many points of view today on electronic money and banking. New products are being designed to challenge the use of currency and checks in millions of routine consumer transactions. Other new systems may allow payments or banking instructions to be sent over networks such as the Internet, which is unprecedented in providing versatile, low-cost communication capabilities. Again, as in the 1970s, articles are being written and conferences are being held to pronounce the end of paper. They may again prove premature.

The payment systems of the United States present a paradox. Our systems and banking arrangements for handling high-value dollar payments are all electronic and have been for many years. Banking records, including those for loans and deposits, have been computerized since the 1960s. Securities markets also now rely on highly automated records and systems, born out of necessity following the paperwork crisis of the 1970s.

Yet in transactions initiated by consumers, paper—currency and checks—remains the payment system of choice. Debit and ATM cards, along with Automated Clearing House payments, account for a very small percentage of transactions. Even the use of popular credit cards has only recently begun to challenge paper's dominance.

Brand names used for many new electronic payment products are designed to suggest analogies to paper currency and coins. It is not

Alan Greenspan is Chairman of the Federal Reserve Board. This paper was presented at the U.S. Treasury Conference on Electronic Money & Banking: The Role of Government, Washington, D.C., September 19, 1996. A title and section heads have been added by the editor.

surprising, therefore, that they sometimes evoke comparisons to an earlier period in U.S. history when private currencies circulated widely. We should, of course, recognize the limitations of this particular experience for drawing policy conclusions relevant to the present. Many of the new electronic payment products are more similar to conventional products, such as debit cards, than to currency. And certainly, the U.S. financial system has evolved considerably since the era of private currency. Thus the baseline from which innovation and experimentation is occurring is doubtless different today. Nonetheless, evaluations of that period can clearly add to our perspective.

Insights from the Free Banking Era

Throughout much of the 19th century, privately issued bank notes were an important form of money in our economy. In the pre–Civil War period, in particular, the federal government did not supply a significant portion of the nation's currency. The charter of the Bank of the United States had not been renewed, and there was no central banking organization to help regulate the supply of currency. Notes issued by state-chartered banks were a major part of the money supply. This was a result, in large part, of the "free banking" movement, a period when state chartering restrictions on banks were significantly loosened. Free banking dominated the landscape in most of the states in the Union starting in the 1830s, and lasted until the National Banking Act was adopted in 1863.

The free banking period was a controversial one in U.S. history. The traditional view has been that this period gave rise to "wildcat banking," in which banks were created simply to issue worthless notes to an unsuspecting public who would seek in vain among the "wildcats" for redemption in specie. Non-par clearing of bank notes, along with suspension of specie payments by banks and outright defaults, did lead to risks and inefficiencies.

But more recently, some scholars have suggested that the problems of the free banking period were exaggerated. Retrospective analyses have shown, for example, that losses to bank note holders and bank failures were not out of line with other comparable periods in U.S. banking history.

The newer research also suggests that, to a degree, the problems of free banking had little to do with banking. In particular, although free banking laws varied considerably by state, issuers of bank notes were often required to purchase state government bonds to back the notes they issued. In some cases, these securities were valued at par rather than at market prices—a structure that evidently did foster wildcat banking. Moreover, no matter what the regulatory valuation scheme, when the state government ran into financial problems, as many often did, both the bonds and the bank notes sank in value. In some cases, this contributed to bank failures.

In the pre–Civil War period, when the general ethos of laissez faire severely discouraged government intervention in the market economy, private regulations arose in the form of a variety of institutions, which accomplished much of what we endeavor to do today with our elaborate system of government rule making and supervision. In particular, scholars have noted that the period saw the development of private measures to help holders of bank notes protect themselves from risk. As the notes were not legal tender, there was no obligation to accept the currency of a suspect bank, or to accept it at par value; accordingly, notes often were accepted and cleared at less than par. As a result, publications—bank note reporters—were established to provide current information on market rates for notes of different banks based on their creditworthiness, reputation, and location, as well as to identify counterfeit notes. Bank note brokers created a ready market for notes of different credit quality. In some areas, private clearinghouses were established, which provided incentives for self-regulation.

Banks competed for reputation, and advertised high capital ratios to attract depositors. Capital to asset ratios in those days often exceeded one-third. One must keep in mind that then, as now, a significant part of safety and soundness regulations came from market forces and institutions. Government regulation is an add-on that tries to identify presumed market failures and, accordingly, substitute official rules to fill in the gaps.

To be sure, much of what developed in that earlier period was primitive and often ineffectual. But the financial system itself was just beginning to evolve.

Reliance on Private Market Self-Regulation

From today's presumably far more sophisticated view of such matters, we may look askance at what we have often dismissed as "wildcat banking." But it should not escape our notice that, as the international financial system becomes ever more complex, we, in our regulatory roles, are being driven increasingly toward reliance on private market self-regulation similar to what emerged in more primitive forms in the 1850s in the United States.

As I have said many times in the past, to continue to be effective, governments' regulatory role must increasingly assure that effective risk management systems are in place in the private sector. As financial systems become more complex, detailed rules and standards have become both burdensome and ineffective, if not counterproductive. If we wish to foster financial innovation, we must be careful not to impose rules that inhibit it. I am especially concerned that we not attempt to impede unduly our newest innovation, electronic money, or more generally, our increasingly broad electronic payments system.

The Flexibility to Experiment

To develop new forms of payment, the private sector will need the flexibility to experiment, without broad interference by the government. The history of the Automated Clearing House provides a useful caution. The Federal Reserve, in partnership with the banking industry, has taken a leading role in developing the ACH system for more than 20 years. It was the advent of the ACH that led many economists to discuss money in a "cashless society." Although the ACH has allowed the automation of some important types of payments, it has never been widely used by consumers.

This experience suggests that creating new technology and providing an interbank electronic clearing system were easy. But developing electronic payment products based on this technology that were more convenient and cost effective than paper, from the standpoint of both consumers and merchants, turned out to be difficult. In our enthusiasm over new electronic payment systems, we significantly underestimated the convenience of paper for consumers and especially the cost and difficulty of building a broad-based infrastructure to support new electronic payment systems. It is also possible that efforts by the government to choose and support a single technology—the ACH in this case—may have slowed efforts by the private sector to develop alternative technologies.

In the current period of change and market uncertainty, there may be a natural temptation for us—and a natural desire by some market participants—to have the government step in and resolve this uncertainty, either through standards, regulation, or other government policies. In the case of electronic money and banking, the lesson from the ACH is that consumers and merchants, not governments, will ultimately determine what new products are successful in the marketplace. Government action can retard progress, but almost certainly cannot ensure it.

Before we set in stone a series of rules for this emerging new medium, let us recall that, across many industries in the economy, forecasting the particular direction of innovation has proven to be especially precarious over the generations. As Professor Nathan Rosenberg of Stanford has pointed out, even relatively mature technologies can develop in wholly unanticipated ways.

Our optimum financial system is one of free and broad competition that is presumed to calibrate appropriately the changing value of products to consumers so that the risk-adjusted rate of return on equity measures the success in providing what people want to buy.

This has turned out to be broadly true in practice and supplied regulators with some sense of which products were serving consumers most effectively. This signal may not be so readily evident in the case of electronic money. The problem is seigniorage, that is, the income one obtains from being able to induce market participants to employ one's liabilities as a money. Such income reflects the return on interest-bearing assets that are financed by the issuance of currency, which pays no interest, or at most a below-market rate, to the holder.

Historically when private currency was widespread, banks garnered seigniorage profits. This seigniorage increasingly shifted to the federal government following the National Bank Act, when the federal government imposed federal regulation on bank note issuance, taxed state bank notes, and ultimately became the sole issuer of currency.

Today, there continue to be incentives for private businesses to recapture seigniorage from the federal government. Seigniorage profits are likely to be part of the business calculation for issuers of prepaid payment instruments, such as prepaid cards, as well as for traditional instruments like travelers checks. As a result, in the short term, it may be difficult for us to determine whether profitable and popular new products are actually efficient alternatives to official paper currency or simply a diversion of seigniorage from the government to the private sector. Yet we must also recognize that a diversion of seigniorage may be an inevitable byproduct of creating a more efficient retail payment system in the long run.

Conclusion

The innovations being discussed today can be viewed from a very different perspective than that afforded by the financial system of the 1850s. Unlike the earlier period, we have a well-developed and tested set of monetary and payment arrangements and a strong national currency. Yet, as in the earlier period, industry participants may find that self-policing is in their best interest. We could envisage proposals in the near future for issuers of electronic payment obligations, such as stored-value cards or "digital cash," to set up specialized issuing corporations with strong balance sheets and public credit ratings. Such structures have been common in other areas, for example, in the derivatives and commercial paper markets.

In conclusion, electronic money is likely to spread only gradually and play a much smaller role in our economy than private currency did historically. Nonetheless, the earlier period affords certain insights on the way markets behaved when government rules were much less pervasive. These insights, I submit, should be considered very carefully as we endeavor to understand and engage the new private currency markets of the 21st century.

7

THE FINANCIAL SERVICES REVOLUTION
Scott Cook

The changing nature of money is only one facet of the financial services revolution. In my remarks, I am going to try to paint a larger canvas to cover some of the other areas where change, I believe, is ahead. As with most revolutions, the spark that lights the tinder that creates the flame really only catalyzes forces that are already under way. Technology is similarly just a catalyst at times for fundamental forces already present. Even some of the greatest technology-led revolutions, or allegedly technology-led, really were only made possible because of trends already present. People claim that the printing press helped Martin Luther initiate the Reformation, but, in fact, all the forces were already present.

Forces behind the Financial Services Revolution

So what are those forces in financial services that are already present and that led to the financial services revolution? I'd start with the consumer, and I'd sight two consumer trends in dealing with the financial environment: complexity and self-reliance.

Complexity

Thirty to 40 years ago, most financial decisions were fairly simple. Consumers saved money and got their financial services from banks and insurance agents. When consumers saved, they put it into the bank. When they wanted a mortgage, they went to the same bank. Products were simple; if consumers wanted to save money, there was one product they could put it in, their passbook savings. If they wanted to get a mortgage, they pretty much had one choice: the 30

Scott Cook is Chairman of Intuit, Inc. This paper is based on his luncheon address at the Cato Institute's 14th annual Monetary Conference, May 23, 1996.

year fixed-rate mortgage. When it came to retirement, they depended on Social Security and their private pensions, which could be expected to cover their needs. Life was pretty simple back then. Today, it's totally different.

Today there are a multitude of financial products and services on the market in the United States. There are so many that just counting the number of companies is complex. Mutual funds were created to make investing easy, so consumers wouldn't have to be burdened with picking individual stocks. All consumers would have to do is give their money to a mutual fund and let the fund managers take care of it. Well, today there are more than 7,000 mutual funds alone to choose from, more than the number of listed stocks on the New York Stock Exchange. At least if you buy a company's stock, like Coca Cola, you kind of know what the company makes. But if you buy an aggressive growth fund, you don't have a clue what is involved unless you understand the fund's prospectus, which is written by some lawyer and is usually opaque. And that's just in the investment realm.

On the borrowing side, it's the same thing. There are all types of loan instruments today. Even the once simple home mortgage now has so many flavors and styles and variations that it is difficult for people to make a decision. Indeed, the products are so complex that not even the financial service companies can reliably know what to recommend. Just imagine the situation for us poor consumers. That's complexity.

Self-Reliance

The second trend in the financial environment is that consumers have become much more self-reliant. There was a time, as I mentioned, when major financial decisions were not so important, or they were taken care of by other parties. It used to be, for example, that people depended on their children for retirement security. Which is why in many earlier societies people had large families. Then there was the move to putting trust in the government or in company pension plans for retirement security. Well, today people have to be self-reliant if they want a secure retirement income. The current institutionally provided retirement plans will not cover people's needs upon retirement. A whole generation of Americans will retire in poverty instead of prosperity, because they simply are not preparing for retirement now. They are not saving enough and investing in the right ways to provide for retirement. By the time you get to 55 or 60, it's too late. This is not just a problem in the United States, it's a global problem.

Today more people believe in UFOs than believe that Social Security will take care of their retirement. People don't place their trust in government or company pension plans; they have to be self-reliant. Yet it is difficult to be self-reliant because things are so complex.

Changes in the Regulatory Climate

Another trend in the financial environment is the change in the financial services industry itself. A trend that is 16 years old in the United States and is happening in other countries as well. And that's the trend to deregulate and free the financial services industry to behave like any other company on the planet.

It is stunning to look back at the way the U.S. government regulated financial services and still regulates them. The unraveling of that regulation began with the Monetary Control Act of 1980. Before 1980, it was basically illegal for U.S. banks to invent new products. Government, not the market, determined how often withdrawals could be made, the minimum deposits, and even the interest rates on deposits. About the only thing left for banks to do was to put their brand names on products and put their ads on the air. That's how hemmed in by regulation the financial services industry was. However, the tide has been turning toward the free market, and the financial services industry is much freer today than in the past.

Who were the losers under the old regulatory regime? Well, consumers, particularly when interest rates were such that banks were not allowed legally to offer consumers a market rate of interest. When inflation increased in the 1970s, the interest-rate ceiling on bank deposits caused a shift of deposits to nonbank institutions. Banks literally could not do anything about it because it was illegal for them to respond. Consumers lost, and ultimately banks lost too. Fortunately, much of this regulation has been stripped away and further reform is on the way.

The Role of Technology

Now that we have considered some of the fundamental underpinnings of the financial services revolution, where does technology come in?

What's interesting is that the financial services industry is perhaps the largest industry today where the product is already marvelously automated. Now that has not always been true. Fifty years ago wealth was stored and transmitted physically through gold bars, stock certificates, bank notes, and coins. Large physical distribution networks were required to collect and distribute the means of exchange. Today, the financial services industry is digital. Wealth is no longer stored in physical means, it's stored as bits on mainframe disk drives and transferred electronically. In fact, the largest consumers of mainframe computing power in the world have always been financial institutions. And that's because the factory for financial institutions is essentially the mainframe computer. That's where they make their product.

Now what's interesting is that even though the back ends of financial institutions are wonderfully automated, the front ends are not. The consumer interface is not. Instead, computers and consumers are insulated from each other and separated from each other by a layer of old stuff. The old stuff being physical branches with tellers, telephones, and managers. Personal contact is very good, but consumers often have no direct access to their accounts. What's amazing is that you often have people looking at computer screens and telling the person on the phone what's on the screen. But why should we have bank employees looking at computer screens when bank customers could do the same thing at home and at lower cost?

Here's another interesting observation. If you survey Americans and ask them when they most want to buy financial products and make financial decisions—such as refinancing their mortgages and investing in mutual funds—most working Americans will say at night and on weekends. Indeed, mutual funds that operate 24 hours a day, 7 days a week are finding that the majority of their business comes in during nights and weekends. But when are banks closed? Nights and weekends, with some exceptions on Saturday. Isn't it odd that we have an immensely expensive distribution structure in this country that is closed the very hours customers most want to buy things? Now, it's not that bankers are bad, it's just that the branch system of distribution is so expensive that if banks were to stay open for two shifts, they would go out of business. Again, this illustrates the mismatch between the nature of the product and the nature of consumer demand, and the old stuff in the middle.

Another example of inefficiency is business use of the U.S. postal system. Businesses still use that system heavily for marketing their products. In 1996, there were more than two billion credit card solicitations sent in the mail, even though the response rate on most direct mail pieces is only about 2 percent. A response rate of 3 percent is considered a success. But a 3 percent response rate means 97 percent waste! Can you believe that U.S. businesses spend billions of dollars in mass marketing every year for something that fails 97 percent of the time? The explanation is simple. Mass marketing is when the marketer sells what the marketer wants, when and where the marketer wants to. What's left out is the consumer. So of course it's mostly waste, because most of the time businesses are selling products that consumers don't want.

Technology can make tremendous changes in slashing the costs of marketing and distribution. Technology will make it far more efficient and far more convenient for the consumer. Instead of finding out weeks later that there was an overcharge or some mischarge on your credit card, you can find out within hours if you wish to. Similarly, computer technology will lower costs and increase convenience, allowing people to shop 24 hours a day, 7 days a week from their homes.

But the benefits of technology go beyond just lowering costs and increasing convenience. Let's take the retirement planning problem, for example. Today only a small percentage of Americans can actually afford a real live, unbiased, fair financial planner to help with retirement. Less than 4 percent of the population will pay the thousands of dollars that it takes for a real financial planner to do the job right. So, instead, most people rely on either books or on persons whose business cards say financial planner but who are actually paid through commissions from insurance companies or brokers. In fact, the most frequently consulted financial experts in the country are insurance agents. And while many of those individuals are straightforward, honest, square-shooting people who are looking out for their customers' best interests, there are some who are merely trying to maximize their commissions or win a trip. Unfortunately, consumers often cannot tell which type of person they are dealing with. Moreover, retirement planning is so complex that most people can't do it out of a book. There has to be a better way.

Banks and others have tried to hire legitimate financial planners to help their customers, but the costs are murderous. What Intuit and other companies are doing is trying to use computer technology to lower the costs of financial planning and help consumers. Intuit's Quicken Financial Planner, which we started selling in 1995, guides our customers through a two-hour interview. The program asks questions intended to build an understanding of our customers' financial situations. Quicken asks people about their income, age, retirement plans, expenses, investments, and current retirement benefits. Quicken then presents a graphic analysis of our customers' financial situations and indicates whether they have enough money or whether in some year in the future, before they are likely to die, their money runs out. Our customers can then play "what-ifs" to see what they have to change to become financially secure in their retirement. Quicken also helps customers figure out how to invest their money. Intuit doesn't make specific recommendations, that's not our job. What we help with is portfolio allocation so that people can get the types of returns that they are going to need over a long period.

This financial service will expand the ability of many Americans to plan for their future. Roughly a third of U.S. households already have computers, and Quicken runs on any standard personal computer with Windows. Interestingly, if people get stuck, or want advice, Intuit has included video clips of financial columnist Jane Bryant Quinn, which appear at each point where a customer might have a question. Quinn will explain the topic and give her opinion on what makes sense. In this way computers can help people improve their decision making so that they can deal with the complexity of the financial system, become self-reliant, and achieve good results instead of disappointment and failure.

Quicken is just the start of a flourishing of using the computer to help people make smarter decisions about their finances, whether planning for retirement or financing their children's college education. There are many people working on this new financial software. What Intuit is doing is not unique. We have a lot of competition from firms of all sorts. Competition is fierce, and both the consumer and the efficiency of the marketplace will benefit.

The Role of Government

Another issue related to the financial services revolution is the issue of government involvement in the industry as there is greater acceptance and demand for electronic commerce. A set of governmental consumer safeguards is now in place, but over time those regulations and laws will need updating to deal with an environment that now has a computer link as opposed to just a paper link. And this process is already occurring.

The Federal Reserve Board recently proposed amendments to Regulation E that would permit financial institutions to give, to those consumers who desired it, the required documentation and advice documents electronically, instead of by paper. This regulatory change is not only better because it lowers costs and increases convenience, it's better because businesses can get their messages to customers faster. This increased efficiency, in fact, should be the sole goal of regulation.

In addition, the Fed has proposed changes to preauthorized electronic funds transfers, and the SEC has just recently modified its rules to allow electronic delivery of some of the disclosure documents such as prospectuses. Intuit's Web site is using that rule to allow mutual fund companies to sell mutual funds and distribute prospectuses electronically on-line. Consumers benefit because they can gather information more easily on mutual funds and mutual-fund alternatives.

The Future of Financial Services

Let me now address the topic of money. All of the financial services that I have already discussed work within the existing system of money and banking. In fact, I am reasonably happy with banks running the payments system. Intuit makes heavy use of the existing payments system and is not trying to invent a new one. That's not our business. Instead, we're trying to improve consumers' access to the financial system by allowing them more freedom to move their own money around.

Although money and payment systems embody technology, they are first and foremost social conventions. When Marco Polo visited China, he was most amazed by the widespread use of paper money. In the West, however, it was unimaginable that anyone would trust slips of paper to be valuable. There was a social convention in China that was absent in the West. Today there is a global social convention that causes most people to believe that chunks of plastic and pieces of check paper are valuable. This change only reinforces the idea that payment systems, like languages, are methods of communication between large groups of people.

As a result of being a social convention, payment systems have great inertia; they do not change rapidly. This slowness of change is not due to technical reasons but to human inertia. For example, even after using electronic payments technology for decades, people still pay for the bulk of things with paper checks. (Over the 1994-95 period, the *increase* in the number of checks written each year was greater than the *total* number of consumer electronic bill payments in 1995.) I believe that new payment systems not only emerge slowly, but only when certain, rather strict, conditions exist.

Innovation in the payments system often occurs in small steps rather than in radical leaps. If an existing payments system can be modified so that it can deliver new benefits sought by consumers, it will likely be the winning form of providing the new benefits. So perhaps the best place to look for many of the new payment systems is to look at the existing system and consider how it can be modified to deliver benefits that people sometimes think can only be delivered through radically new systems. I would point here to the modifications being made to the credit-card system (led by Visa, MasterCard, Microsoft, AmEx, and Netscape) that will allow people to secure on-line credit card transactions. Once that system is in place, I think it will become very popular and become the predominant payments system. In part, because it doesn't have to solve the chicken-and-egg problem that bedevils new payment systems.

In conclusion, the biggest benefit of the new technology is that it will improve efficiency in the current payments system. It will do so by lowering costs, increasing convenience, and allowing people to use their current financial products and services more wisely and more conveniently. Electronification, all the way to the consumer and small business, will enable the invention of new kinds of financial services that have never been comprehended before—things that could not exist without the ubiquitous electronic channel. I do not know what those products will be, but I do know that they will be forthcoming and of true value to consumers.

Intuit is working with other companies to push for those innovations, which will be as important as credit cards and money market funds were when they first appeared in the marketplace. I believe we are entering a period of one or two decades of marvelous invention and creativity that will change the financial services universe.

8

NEW PAYMENTS TECHNOLOGY

Rosalind L. Fisher

The Integrity of the Payments System

While there has been much recent press attention to "electronic money" and the role of a host of new entrants into the business, I am proud to say that Visa and, most importantly, its member financial institutions, are playing—and must continue to play—a central role in the introduction and use of those electronic consumer payment services. I say "central role" for two different but equally compelling reasons.

First, Visa and its member banks have a solid track record of developing an array of payment products and services that meet consumer needs, and we are confident of our ability to continue to do so. Second, the integrity of the payment system, and public confidence in it, could be at risk if so-called electronic money becomes nothing more than zeros and ones—digital signals—without the backing and involvement of regulated financial institutions.

The reason Visa and its member financial institutions must be involved in those evolving services has a public policy foundation: the integrity of the payment system and public confidence in it demands that regulated financial institutions be central players. While we must ensure such involvement, we caution that premature government regulation—or the failure to modify existing regulations to accommodate evolving technologies—could chill or halt the delivery of new financial products to consumers.

An Evolutionary Process

Evolving payment systems is the very core of the Visa mission on behalf of its members. In fact, the Visa organization is itself an

Rosalind L. Fisher is Executive Vice President of VisaNet Services for Visa U.S.A.

example of that evolutionary process. By providing payment systems that offer consumers and merchants convenience, security, and utility, Visa and its members have played a vital role in leading beneficial change in the way business is conducted around the world.

New and innovative technology is the underpinning for the evolution of payment systems. The ability of Visa and its member financial institutions to lead those changes has been enabled by our efforts to harness new technologies and leverage their benefits. While the Visa approach relies on technology, it is consumer and market driven. High tech dazzle only adds value when it provides solutions and products that consumers want and need. Visa and its members build products and services that work for their cardholders and merchants based on innovative technology.

Building solutions that work for consumers and merchants means focusing on much more than just technology—it means adding value and convenience to their lives and their businesses. It also means adding value while addressing issues of key importance. Questions of security, risk, and privacy are all crucial factors in the development of payment products and services. Does this product offer security to consumers and merchants alike? Will it protect financial institutions and their customers from risk? Does it offer protection of data and privacy for its users? All of those questions must be answered and addressed before you have a business solution. And all of those factors are the crux of the goals of Visa and its members as we move toward the technology-driven payment systems of the future.

Changing Technology

One of the key technologies that will move our payment system into the future will be that of the integrated circuit chip. Cards embedded with microprocessor chips are often referred to as "smart cards." The microprocessor can be used to store both financial and nonfinancial information. Visa's first application of this chip technology in the United States is a stored-value card that we call Visa Cash. This card is prepaid with a set amount of value loaded onto the microchip and is an alternative to cash for consumers making small purchases, usually those under $20. Visa Cash was first introduced during the 1996 summer Olympic Games in Atlanta. Other pilots are taking place now worldwide—in Australia, New Zealand, Canada, Spain, Argentina, and Colombia.

Stored-value cards will significantly benefit consumers, merchants, and others involved in payment transactions. Consumers will benefit from ease of use, convenience, and increased transaction speed compared to cash and checks. Merchants will benefit from reduced costs as a result of less pilferage, theft and vandalism, and reduced cash handling due to electronic payments.

Not all of the products and services being introduced by Visa and its member institutions are card-based. Electronic or remote banking is one of the most important initiatives in which exploding technology is enabling Visa and its members to build new product offerings that bring great value and benefit to consumers.

To truly benefit consumers, remote banking must first be accessible and easy to use. Choices such as the type of access device and user software must be left to the individual. For that reason, Visa's remote banking subsidiary, Visa Interactive, offers or is developing interfaces to almost every access device imaginable. From simple touch tone phones and screen phones to personal computers, personal digital assistants (PDAs) and interactive television, Visa is offering a myriad of options for member financial institutions to present to their customers.

Remote banking is only one area of on-line services into which Visa and its members are quickly moving. Electronic commerce over open networks such as the Internet is a technology-driven market that is exploding and Visa is working with its members to facilitate this rapidly evolving electronic marketplace.

Meeting the Market's Needs

While many are addressing various aspects of this developing market through exciting technology, Visa is building business solutions to meet that market's needs. Our first initiative in this area is to provide security for payments made over open networks such as the Internet. Regardless of the technology, the real game when transacting business over the Internet is knowing who you're doing business with. The groundbreaking efforts of Visa and Mastercard in working to build a standard for making transactions secure will allow consumers and merchants the confidence and protection they need to use this new commercial arena successfully. This security—and knowing who you're doing business with—will be key to the future of our country's payment system.

Those products and services will be offered by Visa's member institutions, which today are the major providers of payment system services to our nation's consumers. Confidence in those institutions and the payment services they provide is high, and for good reason. They are regulated by the federal financial institution supervisory agencies and are subject to regular examination by those agencies and state supervisors. Customers' funds are protected by the safety net of federal deposit insurance. As a result of those protections, the public has a high degree of confidence in our members and their products and services, which is essential for economic stability and growth.

Some electronic payment services may be offered through entities that are not subject to the same supervision and regulation as Visa's members. Their customers will not have the protection of the bank supervisory system. Furthermore, to the extent that those entities, as a result of not being regulated by bank supervisors, enjoy a competitive advantage over traditional financial institutions, they may worsen the disintermediation of traditional depositories. For that reason and because of the importance of developing electronic payment systems to the world economy and the importance of preventing abuse in these systems, it is significant to note that a recent report by the European Union's Working Group on EU Payment Systems proposed that only banks be allowed to issue stored-value cards.

Visa also believes that providing new payment products and services through regulated and supervised financial institutions ensures significant safeguards that are not otherwise available. As stored-value cards become an important medium of exchange, policymakers must be cognizant of the potential economic consequences that would result from a loss of public confidence in major unregulated, uninsured issuers. Law enforcement officials combating criminal activities like tax evasion, counterfeiting, and money laundering should consider the potential problems that could result from the development of stored-value card systems that, unlike Visa's, may not generate a well-defined audit trail and could also result from systems whose record-keeping is not subject to periodic supervision and examination. Accordingly, we believe lawmakers should carefully examine the risks that are attendant with participation by these other entities in the payments system.

Avoiding Overregulation

On the other hand, in view of the highly regulated environment in which our members operate and the numerous safeguards that are already in place with respect to depository institutions, we are concerned that additional regulation in this area will stifle the innovations that are being developed. Products and services such as those described here are in nascent stages and could be adversely impacted by overregulation. At the extreme, subjecting many of those products to government regulation could result in their premature death.

The potential application of the Electronic Funds Transfer Act and Regulation E to stored-value cards is an excellent example of this. Regulation E requires that consumers get receipts for electronic funds transfers, such as ATM transactions. If applied to stored-value cards, the product will lose its utility entirely for many of its essential applications. One of the most practical applications of the card will be at vending machines, parking meters and other facilities and merchants geared up to small dollar transactions. Stored-value cards will not be economically viable if machines must be re-engineered to give the user a receipt for a 75 cent soda or 30 minutes at a parking meter.

Also, keeping in mind that one need not have a banking relationship to get a stored-value card, that a name and address are not necessary, and that value on a card may be used quickly, the periodic statement requirements of Regulation E also would destroy the product's utility. We are pleased that the Federal Reserve Board, in its recent proposed revision for Regulation E, has accommodated the special needs of stored-value cards and similar products.

Laws and regulations should not be implemented unless they have been proven to be necessary and can be implemented without imposing excessive costs. Other countries have encouraged innovation by letting products take shape without undue interference. To encourage development and create an environment in which the United States can assume a leadership role in these endeavors, we need to do likewise. Our message is this: Don't add to the regulatory burden of depository institutions. Rather, permit the public to continue to enjoy the benefits of new products and services that Visa and its members are bringing to the market.

9

MONETARY INNOVATION, BANKING, AND REGULATION
Michael N. Castle

The Possibilities of Electronic Money

Coming from the small state of Delaware that has succeeded economically by producing progressive laws that encourage the development of the financial services industry, I am very intrigued by the possibilities of electronic money. My goal has been for Congress to gain an understanding of these new technologies and encourage the sharing of information by industry to avoid the usual inclination of Congress to come to an issue late and then try to rush in and regulate it.

In 1995, my subcommittee, the Domestic and International Monetary Policy Subcommittee of the House Banking and Financial Services Committee, discovered the subject of electronic money and decided that it might be even more fun than a Humphrey Hawkins hearing with Alan Greenspan testifying. During 1995–96, my subcommittee held four hearings on "The Future of Money," designed to introduce Congress and the public to a better understanding of the new monetary technologies that will power the next revolution in world commerce.[1] It was immediately clear that one or more of the schemes underway to create new forms of storing, transmitting, and exchanging value would come under the jurisdiction of my subcommittee, the full Banking Committee, and eventually Congress

---

Michael N. Castle (R-DE) is Chairman of the House Subcommittee on Domestic and International Monetary Policy. This paper is a revised and updated version of his opening address at the Cato Institute's 14th annual Monetary Conference.

[1]Transcripts of the hearings are available from the subcommittee's Web site at http://www.House.Gov/Castle/Banking/.

as a whole.[2] There is nothing like the possibility of grabbing some new turf to get a politician interested in an issue.

Our subcommittee's investigations into this subject have provided an introduction to the emerging electronic technologies and new business opportunities that will drive a worldwide commercial revolution projected to rival the Industrial Revolution. The operative word is projected. Most of the current projections appear to be based less on hard evidence and more on wishful optimism. One projection breathlessly predicts that, by the year 2000, nonbanks will account for as much as 25 percent of the $800 billion in global electronic commerce and payments revenue created by Internet merchants. If that scenario holds true to any significant degree, it is clear that commerce over the Internet, and the electronic means of payment used to facilitate that commerce, will dwarf even widespread penetration of stored-value cards. In this superheated atmosphere, it is hardly surprising to see overnight fortunes created on the strength of the barely tested ideas of very young people.

Hearings on the Future of Money

The first hearing, held on July 25, 1995, involved private-sector entrepreneurs in the field who outlined the potential impact of new technology on future payment systems, the money supply, security, and regulatory compliance issues.

At the second hearing, on October 11, 1995, the subcommittee received testimony from federal entities responsible for law enforcement and management of the monetary system. While the new technology has the potential to revolutionize electronic commerce, law enforcement agencies are concerned about how those same technologies will complicate their missions to counter tax evasion, money laundering, counterfeiting, and fraud.

Regulators accept that monetary policy may be affected by some systems of electronic cash substitutes, that the money supply may be affected, and that some technologies may bring an inflationary potential with them, but they are still willing to wait and watch before calling for regulation. One parochial concern of the Treasury

---

[2]My subcommittee jurisdiction includes oversight of the Federal Reserve System, the World Bank, other international financial institutions, and currency and coinage, including commemorative coins.

is that, as electronic forms of payments become more widespread, the demand for and thus supply of coins and currency will decrease, and so will the revenue raised by the seigniorage from circulating currency, currently $20 billion each year.

Philip Diehl (1995), the director of the U.S. mint, said he expected to be making legal tender stored-value cards before he minted a new one-dollar coin. I do not know if this is good news or bad news, but it has become clear to me that few things are changing as rapidly as is the climate for applications of new technology on the eve of the millennium. In fact, the Fed has already disclaimed any interest in producing legal tender stored-value cards at this time for fear of stifling private-sector initiatives. Without attempting to pass legislation now, Congress should also learn as much as possible about this business and its offshoots.

The third hearing, on March 7, 1996, explored the strategies both banks and nonbanks are employing to profit from the opportunities and challenges presented by these new technologies. Security First Network Bank, FSB, one of several operating banks that primarily exist on the Internet, displayed computer graphics from its Web site. It hopes to create the McBank franchise of the Internet.

We also learned that nonbank institutions are seizing opportunities to perform bank-like functions in what is currently a regulatory near-vacuum. Coley Clark, corporate vice president of Electronic Data Systems, sounded one of the few notes of caution. He believes that consumers will tend to resist technology until there is a persuasive reason for them to adopt it.

Bill R. Norwood, executive director of the Card Application Technology Center of Florida State University, told us about the FSUCard, a multipurpose stored-value and account-access card used by FSU students. FSU has pioneered the multiple-use card and moved from a closed campus environment into the community as well. Students use the card as an I.D., to access dorms, computer systems, and university accounts, including financial aid and tuition payments. It provides access to bank accounts via the ATM system, and it has a stored-value component that permits its use for cashless, low-value transactions. This includes vending machines, copiers, laundry facilities, calling-card functions, and access of voice mail. Tallahassee merchants have petitioned to be admitted into the system to gain access to the nearly 30,000 card holders. Parents love this card because when they fund it they receive a detailed print-out of all their children's college expenditures.

I am convinced that important consumer interests will ultimately provide impetus for whatever legislation is forthcoming. Security of information is a prime consumer interest both here and in Europe. Transactions will need to be verifiable and controllable from the consumer's point of view. These issues and the response of the market to concerns such as purchase satisfaction guarantees, loss replacement, and personal profile data-base management will be important elements to propel the industry or provoke a legislative reaction. If industry leaders are as nimble and intelligent as they are depicted in the business pages, these problems will be anticipated. Access to valuable personal data on purchasing habits will be paid for with whatever currency suits the task, be it frequent flier miles, gasoline coupons, discounts, or twofers. One current example of privacy selling being tested in San Francisco is that, if you make a local telephone call on certain pay phones, you will be invited to listen to a 30 second commercial in return for a free call.

With sufficient time, technology may be able to answer many of the questions being asked about privacy. Biometric data encrypted on stored-value cards could render them worthless to anyone but the rightful owners. New computer applications such as no-toll, full-duplex telephone conversations via the Internet could launch a new wave of personal computer acquisition and usage.

Private-sector practice should move to establish, by contract, convenient forums for resolving commercial disputes on the Internet that might otherwise involve the conflict of several legal systems. This process is already well underway. One center of research into these topics is the Virtual Magistrate Project for rapid arbitration and settlement of on-line disputes. It is being undertaken by the Cyberspace Law Institute (CLI) and the National Center for Automated Information Research (NCAIR). The genie is truly out of the bottle.

The fourth hearing was held on June 11, 1996, with U.S. and international witnesses invited from business and government. At this hearing, we examined the prospects for international private sector agreement, assuming that the window of opportunity for such agreement remains open.

The Bureaucratic Imperative to Regulate

Future congressional hearings on electronic money and commerce are likely to be driven by specific perceived threats to consumer protection and to the integrity of the monetary system, as well as by the threat of new variations of fraud or other criminal behavior. In this atmosphere there is a possibility that much restrictive legislation will be passed. The reflexive reaction of a regulator confronted by something new is first, to establish jurisdiction, then to protect the public from it.

We are being crowded by the future. The concept of money is rapidly changing from the concrete to the electronic, from government issue to commercially created. Digital forms of money hold enormous potential both for expanded commerce and for mischief.

I believe that private-sector industry groups around the world should consult and start building a common agenda. Standards are needed for interoperability, privacy, security, financial responsibility, and especially consumer rights. Otherwise, the natural bureaucratic imperative to regulate will assert itself and much of the promise of the new technology will be lost.

Reference

Diehl, P. N. (1995) "Statement of Philip N. Diehl, Director, United States Mint, before the House Subcommittee on Domestic and International Monetary Policy, 'The Future of Money,'" 11 October.

10

FINANCIAL REGULATION IN THE INFORMATION AGE

R. Alton Gilbert

Several groups are attempting to develop new arrangements for making payments by means of stored-value cards and over the Internet. In this article, I examine the implications of these developments for the safety and soundness of the payments system.[1] One type of threat to safety and soundness involves the nature of the technology used in these new payment arrangements. In particular, will the arrangements be reliable or will they be vulnerable to fraud or attack over computer systems? This article does not deal with these issues raised by the new payments technology. Instead, this article deals only with the role of the government in limiting the vulnerability of the payments system to shocks resulting from default by providers of payment services on their payment obligations.

Some of the firms developing new payment arrangements are not banks. This article examines the implications of entry into the payments business by the nonbank firms whose liabilities are used or will be used for making payments, if their plans are successful. The Appendix describes the services of two of these nonbank providers of payment services. Entry of these firms into the payments business raises some important issues for public policy. Should the new providers of payment services whose liabilities are being used for making payments be supervised and regulated as banks? Is it important,

---

R. Alton Gilbert is Vice President and Banking Advisor of the Federal Reserve Bank of St. Louis. The views expressed in this paper are those of the author, and do not necessarily reflect those of the Federal Reserve Bank of St. Louis or the Federal Reserve System.

[1]See the Appendix for a description of the new payment arrangements.

71

for preserving stability of the payment system, that they be granted access to the discount window?

I investigate these issues by examining banking history. While the technology involved in processing payments has changed over time, issues involving the role of the government in ensuring the safety and soundness of the payments system have remained the same. Lessons drawn from history are still relevant for the entry by non-bank firms into the payments business.

Definition of Supervision and Regulation

Since financial institutions are subject to various forms of regulation, it is necessary to define what I mean by supervision and regulation. My definition reflects the practice of supervision in the United States:

- Supervisors restrict the types of assets in which firms under their jurisdiction may invest.
- Through examinations supervisors assess the quality of the firms' assets and the capacity of their managers to manage risk.
- Supervisors have authority to require changes in the behavior of firms, including authority to require them to increase their capital or cease operations.

The Market Discipline Argument for Exemption from Supervision and Regulation

One argument for exempting nonbank providers of payment services from supervision and regulation rests on the assumption that market discipline will ensure the safety and soundness of the payments system. This market discipline argument rests on the following four assumptions:

1. Market discipline will force the nonbank providers of payment services to hold cash to satisfy the demands of their customers who wish to cash out of their payment systems.
2. These nonbank firms will arrange credit lines with banks to guarantee that they always have access to enough cash to meet their commitments. The banks offering credit lines will impose market discipline on the activities of those firms.
3. Nonbank providers of payment services will limit their investments to high quality earning assets, to maintain the confidence of their customers.

4. Customers would be able to distinguish accurately among payment providers on the basis of the risk they assume. Failure of one nonbank provider of payment services would not undermine customer confidence in the other nonbank providers; failure would not trigger contagious runs by the customers of the other nonbank providers of payment services.

Are these assumptions valid? Is there evidence to support them? Such evidence must be derived from examining periods with a variety of experience with payment-system stability, and a variety of relationships among providers of payment services. In the history of banking in the United States, the relevant period is that prior to formation of the Federal Reserve System in 1913.

Lessons from Banking History

Major institutions in this history are clearinghouses, which functioned somewhat like central banks (Timberlake 1984). Banks formed clearinghouses for efficient clearing and settlement of payments. Operation of clearinghouses required a great deal of cooperation among their member banks, especially during periods of financial crises. Clearinghouses engaged in activities similar to supervision and regulation of their member banks, to ensure that the financial condition of each member warranted support during a financial crisis (Gorton and Mullineaux 1987).

During occasional financial crises, bank customers attempted to withdraw their deposits in the form of currency. Banks attempted to cope with these large cash withdrawals through mutual support coordinated through their clearinghouses. Banks loaned their cash reserves to the clearinghouse member banks experiencing the greatest difficulty coping with depositor withdrawals. Clearinghouses created special certificates during crisis periods (called loan certificates) that the members agreed to accept in settlement through their clearinghouses. This arrangement freed banks to use their cash reserves to meet the demands of depositors, rather than holding inventories of reserves for settlement at the clearinghouse. The discount window of the Federal Reserve was modeled after these actions of clearinghouses during banking panics. Clearinghouses were effective in limiting the effects of bank runs during some banking panics. On other occasions, actions of the clearinghouses were not adequate to deal with panics, and banks resorted to suspension of cash payments to their depositors, which were major disruptions in the operation of the payments system.

To understand why banks attempted to deal with panics through cooperative actions, it is necessary to understand the conflict between the interest of banks as individual organizations and banks as a group during a crisis. The best actions for an individual bank would be to meet the liquidity needs of its customers while keeping its cash reserves as high as possible, and refuse to lend to other banks. Loss of public confidence in a competing bank might drive the bank out of business. Actions by individual banks to guard their own cash reserves, however, would make the crisis worse. It is in the interest of banks as a group that each use its cash reserves to meet the demands of its depositors and lend to the banks having the greatest difficulty meeting the demands of their customers. Through such actions banks might be able to restore confidence of the depositors at all banks in the community.

I draw the following conclusions from this period of United States banking history:

1. Banks were vulnerable to runs by their depositors. Runs by depositors on some banks tended to undermine the confidence of the depositors of other banks.
2. Banks acted cooperatively through their clearinghouses in attempting to deal with such crises. Each bank benefited if all banks in its community could meet the demands of their depositors for cash, since depositor runs that closed one bank were likely to induce depositors to run on other banks (Dwyer and Gilbert 1989, Roberds 1995).
3. Clearinghouses that included as members all of the providers of payment services in their communities were more effective in dealing with banking panics than the clearinghouses that excluded substantial numbers of payments providers (Tallman and Moen 1995).
4. Speed of actions by clearinghouses in dealing with panics was essential to success. Government sanction made such actions more effective (Roberds 1995).
5. Conflicts of interest among banks as competitors may have limited the effectiveness of clearinghouses in dealing with financial crises. In particular, conflicts of interest may have

limited the willingness of the members of the clearinghouses to commit their resources to ensure that their competitors were able to meet the demands of their customers for cash. Conflicts of interest may have limited the speed of response by clearinghouses when banks faced contagious runs by depositors (Goodhart 1985).

One basis for challenging these conclusions is that banking panics were more frequent and their effects more severe in the United States than in other countries. Michael Bordo (1990) documents this difference in the frequency of panics across countries and attributes the relatively high frequency of panics in United States history at least partially to restrictions on branch banking in the United States. This perspective would tend to undermine the relevance of United States banking history as the basis for determining the validity of assumptions that underlie the market discipline argument. Another challenge involves evidence that free banking systems (those that operated without central banks or government supervision and regulation) were more stable than systems with central banks and government supervision and regulation (White 1984).

While a thorough comparison of banking history in the United States and other countries is beyond the scope of this article, the following observations support the relevance of these lessons from United States banking history for current policy analysis. *First,* while banking panics were less frequent in other countries, they did occur. The last banking panic in England occurred in 1866, but after that episode, the Bank of England accepted its role as the nation's lender of last resort (Wood and Gilbert 1986). *Second,* one explanation for the occurrence of banking panics in the United States long after they had ended in other countries is that, because of an unusual ideology involving the government and banking, the United States established the appropriate government policies for dealing with instability in the banking system long after other nations had adopted appropriate monetary arrangements. From this perspective, U.S. history is especially relevant for studying the ability of private firms to achieve stability in the operation of a nation's payment system through private arrangements. *Third,* evidence to support the claim that free banking systems (those without central banks or government supervision and regulation) were stable is subject to conflicting interpretations (Goodhart 1987).

Implications for the Future

Banking history does not support the assumptions that underlie the market discipline argument. Experience indicates that providers of payment services *are* vulnerable to runs by their depositors. While market discipline of banks is important for enhancing the effectiveness of supervision, there are limits to what can be accomplished through market discipline alone. Market discipline and market mechanisms for allocating reserves *are not* effective in preventing crises in the operation of the payments system, or in dealing with crises when they occur. In addition, private associations of nonbank providers of payment services would not be effective in ensuring the stability of their operations.

Banking history illustrates the importance of a central authority for preserving stability of a payments system. To be effective, a central authority must be empowered to act quickly in injecting reserves into providers of payment services in an emergency situation. Its actions must not be hindered by conflicts of interest among providers of payment services. In our payments system that central authority is the Federal Reserve System.

On the basis of U.S. banking history, I conclude that all firms that offer liabilities used by the public for making payments should be required to obtain bank charters. These firms would be supervised and regulated as banks, and have access to the discount window to help them deal with occasional liquidity problems.[2]

---

[2]This view is consistent with a conclusion by the European Union that issuance of general-purpose, stored-value cards should be restricted to deposit-taking institutions. See Report to the Council of the European Monetary Institute (1994).

One basis for challenging the conclusion that providers of payment services should be supervised and regulated as banks involves experience of the public with nonbank issuers of travelers checks and money orders. Participation of these nonbank firms in the payments business does not appear to create problems for the operation of the payments system. The problem with this challenge is that the nonbank issuers of travelers checks and money orders are regulated by state governments to ensure the safety and soundness of their operations. The nature of this regulation is similar to bank supervision and regulation, including the licensing of these money transmitters, restrictions on investments, periodic reports, and on-site examinations (see Levine 1993, Boyles 1996). Stability of the payment system in the presence of nonbank issuers of these payment instruments reinforces, rather than contradicts, the arguments for the general nature of the relation between the government and providers of payment services presented in this article.

I do not think that it is necessary to apply this prescription at this time to all such firms. Currently, there is a lot of research and development in the payments system, and the dollar amounts of payments settled through the new arrangements are small. The government should limit its actions that would discourage this research and development. Stored-value cards and electronic payments for households may become important elements of our payments system, or they might fail to attract the interest of substantial numbers of consumers.

While I do not know the outcome of these experiments, I can predict the nature of the relation between the government and providers of payment services in the future. The firms whose liabilities are used for making payments will have bank charters, will be supervised and regulated as banks by government agencies, and will have access to the discount window. This is my prescription for what this future relationship *should* be, and my prediction of what it *will* be. We may get to this future through deliberate planning, or through some future crises in the operation of new entrants to the payments business. History includes many examples of crises in the operations of firms that provide payment services leading to changes in their relation to the government. The challenge for government policy involves choosing a path to this future that facilitates innovation while limiting the potential trauma for those who begin using the new arrangements for making payments.

Appendix: Nonbank Providers of Payment Services

Firms that issue *stored-value cards* encode the cards with monetary value which customers use for making purchases at vending machines and retail outlets equipped with card readers. Use of such cards for vending machines is common on university campuses. One of the nonbank providers of payment services is National Cashe-Card, of St. Louis, Missouri. This firm provides identification cards for students at Washington University, located in St. Louis. Students who wish to use the cards for purchases at vending, copying, and washing machines first load value on the cards at terminals on campus. Value recorded on the cards is reduced each time a student uses a card in a machine.

When a student loads value on a card, by injecting currency into a terminal or debiting a transactions account at a depository institution, the transactions account of National CasheCard at a federally insured depository institution is credited. National CasheCard pays vendors and provides any student refunds out of that transactions account. Students and vendors rely on National CasheCard to honor its payment obligations out of that transactions account. Thus, National CasheCard offers payment services through a deposit account at a bank. The bank that offers the transactions account does not accept responsibility for honoring those payment obligations. National CasheCard offers to license its system to banks or their payment associations.

A service planned by CyberCash called "Electronic Coin" involves *payments transmitted over the Internet.* To receive electronic coins, customers send money to CyberCash and receive coins transmitted over the Internet that are stored in their computer, in the form of digits recognized in the Cybercash system as monetary value. According to the plans of CyberCash, customers of its Electronic Coin service will be able to make purchases over the Internet. A customer who sees a product on the Internet he wishes to buy will transmit the coins to the merchant over the Internet. The merchant, in turn, will transmit the coins to CyberCash.

CyberCash will deposit the money received from purchasers of Electronic Coins in transactions accounts at federally insured depository institutions, and make payments to merchants out of those accounts. Thus, CyberCash, which is not a bank, plans to offer payment services to its customers through use of deposit accounts at banks. The electronic coins, which will be assets of CyberCash customers, will be liabilities of CyberCash.

A rival system for payments over the Internet, DigiCash, involves different relations among this service provider, customers, and banks. DigiCash licenses its Internet payments system to banks. The monetary value in computers available for purchases over the Internet is the monetary liability of the banks that license the system from DigiCash. Integrity of this part of the payment system does not depend on the cash management practices of DigiCash.

References

Bordo, M.D. (1990) "The Lender of Last Resort: Alternative Views and Historical Experience." Federal Reserve Bank of Richmond *Economic Review* 76 (January/February): 18–29.

Boyles, D. (1996) Testimony before the Subcommittee on Domestic and International Monetary Policy of the Committee on Banking and Financial Services, U.S. House of Representatives, 11 June.

Dwyer, G.P. Jr., and Gilbert, R. A. (1989) "Bank Runs and Private Remedies." Federal Reserve Bank of St. Louis *Review* 71 (May/June): 43–61.

Goodhart, C.A.E. (1985) *The Evolution of Central Banks: A Natural Development?* London: London School of Economics and Political Science.

Goodhart, C.A.E. (1987) "Review of *Free Banking in Britain: Theory, Experience and Debate, 1800–1845*" by L.H. White. *Economica* 54 (February): 129–31.

Gorton, G., and Mullineaux, D. (1987) "The Joint Production of Confidence: Endogenous Regulation and Nineteenth Century Commercial-Bank Clearinghouses." *Journal of Money, Credit and Banking* 19 (November): 457–68.

Levine, E.C. (1993) "The Regulation of Check Sellers and Money Transmitters." *National Association of Attorneys General* (March/April): 12–13.

Roberds, W. (1995) "Financial Crises and the Payments System: Lessons from the National Banking Era." Federal Reserve Bank of Atlanta *Economic Review* 80 (May/June): 15–31.

Tallman, E.W., and Moen, J. (1995) "Private Sector Responses to the Panic of 1907: A Comparison of New York and Chicago." Federal Reserve Bank of Atlanta *Economic Review* 80 (March/April): 1–9.

Timberlake, R.H. Jr. (1984) "The Central Banking Role of Clearinghouse Associations." *Journal of Money, Credit and Banking* 16 (February): 1–15.

White, L.H. (1984) *Free Banking in Britain: Theory, Experience and Debate, 1800–1845.* New York: Cambridge University Press.

Wood, G.E., and Gilbert, R.A. (1986) "Coping with Bank Failures: Some Lessons from the United States and the United Kingdom." Federal Reserve Bank of St. Louis *Review* 68 (December): 5–14.

Working Group on EU Payment Systems (1994) *Report to the Council of the European Monetary Institute on Prepaid Cards.* European Monetary Institute, Frankfurt-am-Main, Germany.

11

THE NEW MONETARY UNIVERSE AND ITS IMPACT ON TAXATION

Richard W. Rahn

Moving money at the speed of light to any place in the world anonymously over the Internet will soon be as easy as a few keystrokes on your business or home computer. Such anonymous monetary movements substantially increase the potential that the size of the identifiable tax base will be diminished. Government tax authorities are both challenged and threatened by this new technology. As expected, there are some at the U.S. Treasury and the Department of Justice who are proposing regulations, essentially requiring every American business and individual to report every item of income or expenditure worldwide, through electronic means, to the government. Not even the Nazis or communists were able to achieve this level of proposed intrusiveness. Fortunately, many in the new Congress are set to oppose this latest attempt to deny us any remnant of financial privacy.

We are now at a crossroads. The new technologies are going to enable many American businesses and investors to pick up and leave—electronically. The more the government tries to tax, regulate, control, and confiscate, the greater the incentive for business and investors to leave.

The State of the Technology

Electronic transfers greatly reduce transaction costs and the possibility of loss. Americans are now starting to pay their bills by using credit cards and inexpensive "Smart Phones." These systems provide customers with a full record of income and payments: good

---

Richard W. Rahn is President of Novecon Ltd. and Novecon Management Co., L.P.

for record-keeping, but bad for privacy. In fact, the IRS is already working on a system to gather financial information electronically and prepare tax returns. That might crimp the tax lawyers and accountants a bit, but the Big Brother police state aspects are at least as unpalatable.

There are, however, technological alternatives to blind submission to the state. Experiments are now under way. One is called "e-cash," operating in Amsterdam by a company named DigiCash. The electronic version of the anonymous paper dollar is now with us. Individuals will be able to move their funds around the world, literally at the speed of light, from one bank to another or to a creditor, without the bank knowing to whom the money was paid, or the creditor knowing from which bank or even country the money came.

Another experiment is the Mondex system in Swindon, England. Under this system, which has many of the same anonymous features of the DigiCash system, payments can also be made outside the banking system—directly from card to card (by smart card reader/writers).

Through the use of cryptographic technology (scrambled numbers for personal codes), the ease of conducting electronic transactions would be combined with the elegant anonymity of paying in cash. The two most important features of the "e-cash" system—security and anonymity—will be ensured by using cryptographic digital signatures to establish the authenticity of the payer, while at the same time assuring his anonymity and untraceability. The virtual electronic dollar bills will, at the same time, be assigned individual electronic serial numbers, which will also be checked for authenticity. The bank will know how much to pay and what code to pay it to, but will not know the owner of the receiving code, hence the payee too remains anonymous.

Naturally, the IRS doesn't like it. But the matter may be beyond its control. Soon, Americans will be offered two competing versions of the future. The first is the society in which all transactions can be monitored by the government (and other interested parties). The second is where individuals can choose which transactions will be made available to curious eyes, and which will remain anonymous. (Individuals do run the risk of not being able to prove they paid their bills under some of the anonymous systems.)

The View of the Future

Many in the government and other organizations will argue for a ban on anonymous systems, contending that such capabilities benefit primarily drug traffickers, money launderers, assorted terrorists, and plain old tax dodgers. Libertarians, on the other hand, will warn of the dangers that accrue when government has almost total scrutiny of individuals. One does not have to envision what a Hitler or Stalin could have done with such a system; just try to imagine the kind of ordeal investigators could inflict on anyone trying to get Senate confirmation for government service.

The fact is that the fears of both sides are correct. But some of the legitimate fears of the government can be mollified by repealing the income tax and substituting low-rate consumption and withholding taxes. While anonymous systems will make detection of criminal activity more difficult, especially as private encryption protocols are developed, current regulations to thwart money launderers and drug dealers are also failing. This fact does not justify imposing further restrictions on legitimate money transfers by honest citizens to the detriment of our civil liberties.

The revolution taking place in electronic money means that banks and other organizations will be able to create their own money for transactional or investment purposes and literally move these moneys around the globe at the speed of light. The definition of money as a government-created legal tender will become less and less relevant. The existing distinctions between money, goods, services, and assets will increasingly disappear as they become more interchangeable. Unfortunately, some will misuse the new technology either with criminal intent or through irresponsibility, causing losses to users. Knowledgeable markets are likely to be a better antidote for wrongful actions than more government regulation.

Definitions of income and money will be increasingly blurred, presenting an impossible task to a tax collector who tries to tax things that can be transformed instantaneously into something else and moved to anywhere in the world with no paper or electronic trail. Public-key cryptography, which has already been developed, means electronic bank notes can be certified without the issuer knowing to whom they were issued. Smart cards used as an electronic purse can have the same anonymity as paper cash.

The electronic age, with virtually instantaneous international financial transactions and with encrypted confidential smart cards substituting for money, will make the taxation of capital transactions, interest, and dividends increasingly problematic. In an age where most people can today transfer money and pay bills with an ordinary telephone, enforcing taxation on these types of transactions will become virtually impossible. The cost of trying to enforce them may well exceed the revenue collected and certainly will exact a price in terms of lost economic efficiency and lost privacy rights that exceeds the benefits of their continued taxation.

Government authorities cannot stop this revolution, because it is a worldwide revolution with too many people having the knowledge. Censorship and regulation will not work because progress in developing the means of evasion will always be far ahead of those who are trying to restrict it. In the same way that most totalitarian governments have largely given up trying to control the flow of information, because technology has made it an impossible task, governments will need to realize that the old central bank monopolies on the issuance of money will also go the way of the buggy whip.

Government officials have two choices: to redesign their tax and monetary systems to reflect technological reality, or to try to create a system in which every investment and every expenditure by every person is known throughout their lives. In the new world of monetary freedom there is no halfway ground. Either the government will know everything, or the government will only know what is voluntarily revealed. An all-knowing government is doomed to fail, practically and politically, and attempts to impose a "Big Brother" government could impoverish the nation and trample our liberties.

Will Tax Evasion Increase?

If taxpayers may easily avoid reporting particular types of income or transactions with virtually no danger of being caught because of technological innovations, then the taxes on those incomes or transactions are, quite literally, voluntary, and will only be paid by conscientious citizens who abide by our tax laws out of a sense of duty and honor rather than the threat of civil or criminal penalties.

The cybermoney revolution makes some forms of tax evasion very easy. Given that it will be increasingly possible to move monies around the world from computer to computer, and in and out of smart cards anonymously, without going through the banking system, as previously mentioned, tax evasion can be accomplished with a few strokes of the keyboard.

A few examples: Assume you are a lawyer in New York doing work for a client in a jurisdiction without an income tax. You do your work in New York but send it via the Internet (electronic mail). The client agrees to pay you in electronic money. As your bills become due, the client sends the money to you over the Internet and it is downloaded into your computer. You in turn pay your bills by sending electronic cash from your computer and by loading up your smart card. And only you—a smart New York lawyer—decide what electronic and paper records both to create and keep. Anyone who can sell their personal services over the Internet—lawyers, programmers, writers, architects, and engineers, for example—will have the same ability. If tax rates are kept low enough, and taxes previously collected from individuals are instead collected at the business level, both incentive and opportunity to evade legitimate taxes will be reduced.

Tax evasion is normally considered a reprehensible crime, and the sanctions are serious for tax evaders in most jurisdictions. But what if the government is totally corrupt (which occasionally occurs with local governments in the United States)? In the United States, it is a crime to provide funds to a criminal organization. If you pay taxes to a governmental unit that is operating essentially as a criminal organization, are you not both violating the law and engaging in immoral behavior? What do you do about a government that is only partially corrupt? Provide only partial tax payments? What do you do when the government is not spending the tax money on a cost-effective basis? For instance, assume there is a government program that provides food for the needy, and that there is a private charity that does the same thing for the same people in a less costly and more effective manner. Would not the moral person refuse to pay the government tax, but instead support the private charity to an equal or greater amount?

The point of the above discussion is that if it becomes increasingly easy to avoid taxation, will not many people, who are not criminals in the traditional sense, begin to make their own moral decisions about how much government to support.

Tax Enforcement and Potential Abuse

According to House Ways and Means Committee Chairman Bill Archer, approximately 44 million Americans had an incident with the IRS in 1995. Most often they received deficiency notices. It is well documented that most individuals and businesses pay the requested amount rather than fight the IRS, even though the IRS is very frequently wrong. Why? Because individuals and businesses find it less costly to pay the "bribe" to the IRS than to fight. Bribe is the appropriate word, because many IRS officials are expected to meet quotas (a.k.a. performance standards, or some other politically correct term). Hence, officials are more interested in collecting revenue than administering fairness. Taxpayers know that given the complexity of the tax laws and the cost of fighting the IRS, the deck is stacked in favor of the bureaucratic totalitarians. So, they pay protection money to avoid an even more costly audit or legal suit.

Most Americans were appalled when they learned the extent to which paid informants were used by the communists to "protect the state." Yet, increasingly in our own country the government relies on paid informants to report on the alleged tax, environmental, or other misdeeds of businesspeople. Thus, the incentive is to make charges without sufficient evidence. Unfounded charges can easily destroy the reputation and financial well being of an individual or business. The difference between the action of the U.S. government and the former communist East German secret police is a matter of degree, not form.

Most Americans are not aware of the broad powers that the government already has to pry into and control their monetary affairs. Much of the recent regulation has been enacted as part of "the war on drugs" and a general attempt to control "money laundering." The Treasury and other government departments have been holding meetings in an attempt to choose the nature and form of regulation that they will impose on what they refer to as "cyberpayments." The goals of the proposed regulations range from the noble to the base. Reasons given for increasing regulation include: "The need for oversight of the soundness and safety of financial institutions"; consumer protection; law enforcement (drugs, etc.); and, of course, taxation. The Financial Crimes Enforcement Network (FinCEN) of the Treasury Department has taken the lead in the effort, to date, to propose regulation of cyberpayments. FinCEN administers the Bank Secrecy Act (BSA) and implements policies to detect and prevent money laundering.

A number of individuals within the regulatory bureaucracy and on policy staffs advocate extending the existing money laundering regulations and BSA provisions to nonfinancial businesses and individuals who engage in "cyberpayments." To understand what this might mean, and the cost and loss of freedom it would entail, it is worth reviewing the present laws and regulations that now primarily affect financial institutions and their employees.

On September 23, 1994, President Clinton signed the Money Laundering Suppression Act of 1994. This Act increases the federal government's BSA oversight of money transmitting businesses that engage in check cashing, currency exchange, money order and traveler's check sales, and money transmitting and remittance services.

The BSA currently requires a person who transports, mails, or ships currency or other monetary instruments in amounts greater than $10,000 into or out of the United States, to complete U.S. Customs Service Form 4790, Report of International Transportation of Currency or Monetary Instruments ("CMIR"). The term "monetary instrument" is defined in the BSA as (i) currency; (ii) traveler's checks in any form; (iii) negotiable instruments (i.e., personal checks, business checks, bank checks, cashier's checks, third-party checks, promissory notes, money orders) that are either in bearer form, endorsed without restriction, made out to a fictitious payee or otherwise in a form that title thereto passes upon delivery; (iv) incomplete negotiable instruments signed but with the payee's name omitted; and (v) securities or stock in a bearer form.

Money transmitters, as defined in the Act, are businesses (other than the United States Postal Service, a securities broker/dealer, or a bank subject to the BSA) that provide check cashing, currency exchange, money transmitting or remittance services, or that issue or redeem money orders, traveler's checks or other similar instruments.

Each money transmitting business registering under this provision must provide the Treasury with the following information:

1. the name and location of the business;
2. the name and address of each person who: (a) owns or controls the business, (b) is a director or officer of the business, or (c) participates in the affairs of the business;
3. the name and address of the depository institution(s) at which the business maintains a transaction account;
4. an estimate of the annual volume of business; and
5. any other information required by Treasury.

Failure to comply with the registration requirements could result in a civil money penalty of $5,000 a day for each violation, a criminal penalty of five years in prison and/or a fine ($250,000 for individuals or $500,000 for corporations) and civil forfeiture. To establish a criminal or civil structuring violation, the government no longer has to prove that the defendant knew structuring itself was illegal.

In addition to the above provisions the Act also amends the BSA to

> expand the definition of a financial institution subject to the BSA to include casinos or gambling establishments with annual gaming revenues of more than $1 million which are: (i) state-licensed casinos; or (ii) Indian gaming operations under the Indian Gaming Regulatory Act.

Other provisions of the Act:

- make it a federal crime to run an illegal money transmitting business that is operating without an appropriate state license and in violation of state law, and provide for the criminal forfeiture of any property involved in the crime;
- provide the Treasury with the authority to issue regulations requiring financial institutions and their officers, directors, and employees to report suspicious transactions relating to possible violations of law or regulations;
- prohibit financial institutions and their directors, officers and employees from notifying any person involved in a suspicious transaction that a suspicious transaction report has been made;
- shield financial institutions and their directors, officers, and employees who report suspicious transactions from civil liability when they report suspicious transactions under any authority to any person;
- require the Treasury and Department of Justice to establish an anti-money laundering training team of experts to assist foreign countries in identifying, investigating and prosecuting violations of money laundering laws;
- preserve an appellate court's jurisdiction over the property subject to forfeiture even if the property has been removed from the jurisdiction;
- provide for the civil forfeiture of identical or "substitute" assets in cases where the property is fungible (e.g., bank accounts);

- allow any party to a civil forfeiture proceeding based on a narcotics, money laundering, or BSA offense to subpoena pertinent financial institution records upon the order of the district court where the forfeiture action is pending;
- permit awards to be paid to informants in cases involving money laundering or structuring transactions to evade the CTR or CMIR reporting requirements;
- add new money laundering predicate offenses, including mail theft, food stamp fraud, violations of the Foreign Corrupt Practices Act and foreign bank fraud, kidnapping, robbery, and extortion;
- make it a crime to structure purchases of monetary instruments to evade the $3000 identification and record-keeping requirements; and,
- provide whistle-blower protection to employees who provide information to the government regarding violations of the BSA or money laundering statutes.

If these and other provisions are extended to nonfinancial institutions and individuals, it is not overstatement to say that Americans will be required to spy on their friends and neighbors—thus ending any sense of personal privacy and financial freedom.

Popular appeals to "wage war" on criminals and drug dealers, as an excuse for improper bureaucratic invasion of legitimate financial privacy, must be resisted. Criminal action can be curtailed without resorting to an invasive government, which history shows inevitably leads to abuse.

Conclusion

The danger is very real, but the battle for financial freedom is not yet lost. To win this battle, advocates of liberty will by necessity need to be involved with tax reform. The abolition of the income tax and its replacement with a low-rate noninvasive tax system will take away much of the rationale for income and expenditure monitoring by the government.

In the age of the cyberpayment, we cannot both keep the present income tax system and enforce it, and at the same time keep our liberty and privacy. We should all work together to get rid of the income tax rather than ridding ourselves of liberty.

12

PRIVACY AND SOCIAL PROTECTION IN ELECTRONIC PAYMENT SYSTEMS

David Chaum

I would like to address what I think is a misunderstood yet very attractive way to create economic growth: electronic consumer payment systems—both for the physical world and cyberspace. To clarify the misunderstanding, I will begin by describing two different scenarios for building electronic payment systems, each scenario having its own shortcomings.

One scenario is a fully traceable world, "Clipper cash," that is, a world of what I would like to call "data fascism." The other straw man is an electronic payments system that mimics the anonymity of paper currency today.

The Data Fascism Scenario

Think tank studies have indicated that making ordinary consumer payments totally traceable by government would be a way to influence society enormously and curtail all kinds of activity, and cause a kind of homogeneity. Technically it is really very easy to do this. Almost all the new emerging electronic payment systems, in fact, already do this, and no really fundamentally new technology is required.

Basically, there are two ways to trace payments, and you can mix and match them as you like. One is with an on-line system: the consumer goes to a point of payment and is required to identify himself by some kind of biometrics, such as a fingerprint; the consumer's account is accessed; and the consumer can then conduct various kinds of transactions. There are central records of all of these

---

David Chaum is the Founder and Managing Director of DigiCash.

91

transactions, and the consumer can be locked out of the system at any moment.

Another way to achieve the same effect, which is a little bit trickier, is to empower chips, individual chips that people can carry around and treat as personal bank branches or offices. Like a "Clipper chip," each chip is a little black box, the inner workings of which are inscrutable to and unmodifiable by its holder. Inside the box are mechanisms that ensure that people do not spend more than they really have or go beyond their line of credit. At least that is what should be in that box, but consumers have no real way of knowing what is actually in that box and what it is doing.

For instance, that box might be sending out encrypted messages revealing everything consumers do, which could be collected by all manner of parties. It might even allow receipt of special messages that cause it to go into a secret mode. This might be used to discriminate against certain types of people or enforce arbitrary rules that have been preprogrammed into the chip or that are downloaded. It's a pretty powerful kind of mechanism. Of course, there is always a lingering doubt on the part of consumers about what is really going on in that box and what it will do in the future. And even just that doubt can have a chilling effect on society. Some countries may wish to adopt this kind of electronic payments system, but I hope the United States is not one of them.

Totally Anonymous Electronic Payments

There is a another extreme scenario, a sort of pure form, and it refers to a totally anonymous payments system. I would like to submit that we already have more or less totally anonymous transactions today through the use of paper currency.

Estimates from major banks indicate that the cost of operating the physical money system is between 2 and 3 percent of gross domestic product. And the extent of counterfeiting, of course, is not even acknowledged by the U.S. government. Apparently some countries do report it and it is staggering. It is a tax on society that is used to foster all kinds of other criminal activity. Clearly not a desirable property of the current payments system. There are also other criminal uses stemming from the use of paper currency—such as various types of extortion, black markets, bribery, tax evasion, and money laundering.

When we move to an electronic consumer payments system, it's a new medium, and a different world than the paper world—it creates different opportunities and different vulnerabilities. So we cannot exactly equal paper cash in an electronic medium. But we can come very close, and I'll take responsibility for publishing some papers in the last decade that told in plain mathematical formulas how to do it, and it is no secret.[1] So, in a sense, the cat is out of the bag.

Achieving Privacy While Protecting Society: The Best of Both Worlds

Neither system, data fascist not perfect anonymity, is very desirable. What is needed is an electronic payments system to create economic growth and prosperity; it must be a common system that will be able to be widely adopted. Hopefully, it will not have the drawbacks of either scenario.

Now the misunderstanding I mentioned stems from the notion that one must choose between the two scenarios. That is a fairly common way of thinking. However, my research in cryptography over the last decade and a half has taught me that cryptography is extraordinarily powerful. As an illustration, let me explain how we can actually obtain the best of both scenarios.

That result is achieved through the blind-signature technology. Systems based on it are now being launched by Deutsche Bank and other major banks in European countries, and we have it on chip cards and in electronic wallets. The essential idea is simply that instead of receiving digital money from your bank, which you withdraw just like paper money, your computer actually participates in creating the money and actually chooses the serial numbers for you at random. Those serial numbers are then hidden by your computer in a layer of blinding (a special kind of encryption) for which only your computer knows the key. Next, you submit those blinded numbers to the bank for a signature; the bank signs them, to make them worth an equivalent value that it has taken from your account; and, when you receive them back, you can remove the layer of blinding. Thus, when you spend those digital coins, everyone can see that they are signed by the bank, and the bank has to honor

---

[1]See, for example, Chaum (1981, 1989). A summary and update of my earlier work can be found in Chaum (1992).

them (at least the first time each is spent), but no one, not even the bank, can know which account the money was withdrawn from. Thus, privacy is preserved.

But, since your computer knows the serial numbers of the coins it has created, it can always cooperate with the bank to allow tracing of a coin to the recipient's account. This means the payer can always retroactively and irrefutably reveal the recipient of the funds. With such electronic cash, the various criminal uses—extortion, black markets, bribery—are no more likely than they are with checks today. (After all, what kidnapper would accept payment by check?)

Not only can the recipient always be traced by the payer, but the money has to be deposited into a bank account in order to be verified as valid. Thus, the total revenue received by any entity would be known almost in real time, thereby preventing the hiding of income for tax evasion and many types of money laundering.

Conclusion

Fear of technology is often cited as an inhibitor of its adoption. I think that what will prevent information technology from being fully adopted, and making its best contribution to economic growth, will be fear that personal information may be misused. This impediment must be overcome before we can achieve the full potential of this new medium.

My personal goal is to try to build a payments system that can be widely adopted and that will stimulate economic growth both in cyberspace and in the physical world. The system I envision will also help alleviate many social problems and act as a springboard for increasing individual freedom. All this will come about as consumers realize that the use of electronic payments media does not have to compromise their privacy, but in fact can empower them to protect their own interests.

References

Chaum, D. (1981) "Untraceable Electronic Mail, Return Addresses, and Digital Pseudonyms." *Communications of the ACM* 24 (2) (February).

Chaum, D. (1989) "Privacy Protected Payments: Unconditional Payer and/ or Payee Untraceability." In D. Chaum and I. Schaumuller-Bichl (eds.) *Smart Card 2000*: 69–93. Amsterdam: North-Holland.

Chaum, D. (1992) "Achieving Electronic Privacy." *Scientific American* (August): 96–101.

PART III

MONETARY POLICY IN THE INFORMATION AGE

13

E-MONEY: FRIEND OR FOE OF MONETARISM?

George Selgin

Economists, and central bankers especially, are inclined to treat financial innovations as something that makes managing the money stock more difficult, thus increasing the need for monetary discretion. Financial innovations, the argument goes, tend to lead to unpredictable changes in the "money multiplier" or in the demand for particular monetary aggregates or both. Consequently, the more innovations that occur, the less merit there is in monetarist arguments for binding the hands of monetary authorities, making them obey strict rules, and monetary base growth rules in particular. The emergence of new electronic means of payment, or "e-money," is only the latest private financial-market wrinkle to excite the anxieties of central bankers, giving them grounds for asserting their right to improvise.

But there is another way to think of financial innovations, including e-money, that leads to quite opposite conclusions. Financial innovations can often be understood as the private market's way of supplying new and improved alternatives to central-bank issued payments media. The more such innovations succeed, the less the public has to rely on central banks as direct sources of exchange media. And, the less the public has to rely on central banks, the more it can afford to deny such banks discretionary powers. This seems to me to be particularly obvious in the case of e-money.

Privatizing the U.S. Money Stock

For most of this century the Federal Reserve, like most other central banks, has had a monopoly of hand-to-hand currency. Regulations, including a prohibitive tax on state bank notes and bond-collateral requirements for National Bank notes, both dating back

George Selgin is Associate Professor of Economics at the University of Georgia. He thanks Lawrence H. White for his suggestions.

to the Civil War, have long prevented private financial firms from directly challenging the Fed's currency monopoly even when they might have been able to offer more attractive and efficient alternatives—private bank notes were last issued in the United States in the 1930s. The public has therefore had little choice but to allow the Fed the freedom to issue too much money, or bear the consequences of being stuck with too little.

The development of electronic money, and cash cards especially, holds out the promise that the public may one day cease to be hostage to the Fed. E-money amounts to a technological end-around play, circumventing long-standing restrictions on private bank notes. In principle at least, cash and debit cards together could entirely take the place of Federal Reserve notes presently circulating within U.S. borders.[1] The U.S. money stock in public hands would then be fully privatized, with the Fed serving only as a source of bank reserves.

E-Money and the Merits of a Monetary Base Rule

Far from making a strict monetary base rule less workable, such a privatized money stock would make it more workable than ever, because the Fed would no longer have to have the power to adjust the amount of base money in response to changes in the public's demand for cash.

A little algebra helps clarify the argument. As any student of money and banking knows, up to now our monetary system has been one in which the money multiplier—the ratio of total public deposit and currency holdings to the monetary base (the outstanding amount of Federal Reserve notes and bank reserve credits at the Fed)—depends on at least two variables. These are (1) the public's desired currency-to-deposit ratio (c) and (2) the bank's desired reserves-to-deposit ratio (r). The formula for the multiplier is $m = (1 + c)/(r + c)$, where the total money stock, M, is equal to mB, and B stands for the monetary base. In this formula, B is the only thing that the Fed controls with any degree of precision: to expand B by $100 million, the Fed only has to arrange to purchase an equal value of government securities in the open market.

---

[1] An unknown but very substantial part of the outstanding stock of Federal Reserve Notes is held outside the United States. The chances of e-money supplanting such foreign holdings of Federal Reserve Notes seem relatively slim.

The great virtue of a monetary base rule is, therefore, that the Fed could not fail to abide by such a rule except through outright negligence or caprice. In contrast, with any other sort of rule (including a zero inflation rule), the Fed could always appeal to unforeseen changes in factors beyond its control as its excuse for failing to keep its promise.

A long-standing argument against a monetary base rule is that such a rule would not allow the central bank to adjust the base in response to unforeseen changes in the public's desired currency ratio. Historically, changes in the public's desired currency ratio have been a major determinant of both cyclical and seasonal changes in the money stock. Unpredicted changes in that ratio have, in the absence of some offsetting Fed response, led to undesired changes in the money stock, nominal spending, and prices—most notoriously during the banking crises of the early 1930s.[2] The emergence of e-money strengthens the case for a strict monetary base rule by, in effect, helping to eliminate the currency ratio as a factor influencing the money multiplier. The multiplier would then simply be the reciprocal of the banking system reserve ratio. The challenge of monetary control would be simplified accordingly: with one less variable to worry about, the Fed would not need so much freedom to improvise.

That at least would be true if e-money could completely take the place of Federal Reserve notes, making further issues of such notes unnecessary, and allowing the Fed simply to "sterilize" old notes turned in by banks for reserve credits.[3] In fact, with perhaps $100 billion in Federal Reserve notes still circulating within U.S. borders, we have a long way to go before we can afford to shut down the Bureau of Printing and Engraving. In particular, persons who do

[2]Prior to 1933, the public's increased demand for currency did not reflect any general loss of confidence in private circulating exchange media—as evidenced by the widespread use of scrip and by the continued strong demand for National Bank notes. There is every reason to believe, in other words, that some further relaxation of restrictions on bank note issuance would have helped banks to protect their reserves. (The bond-deposit requirements limiting the issuance of National Bank notes were in fact relaxed temporarily, but only enough to allow an extra $230 million in such notes to be issued.) Things changed in early 1933, when rumors of a devaluation led to a run on the dollar.

[3]The Fed could do this by automatically reducing its base-money growth target by the factor $(1-r)$ times the value of returned notes.

not currently have bank accounts, and who could not easily afford digital wallets, may need some encouragement to induce them to make do without greenbacks. Perhaps the government might help things along by equipping needy applicants with free e-wallets, financing the operation with funds diverted from the printing presses. But do not expect the government to jump at this idea: the Treasury stands to lose billions of dollars of revenue from any reform that lessens the demand for government paper money.[4]

Conclusion

Even a thoroughgoing privatization of the money stock is not enough to make a strict (no-feedback) monetary base rule work perfectly. Undesired fluctuations in nominal incomes and prices could still occur as a result of unforeseen changes in bank reserve ratios or the demand for money. But the case for a strict monetary rule has, after all, never been based on the claim that such a rule would be perfect. It is based on the claim that an imperfect rule would be better in practice than any imperfectly used central bank discretionary powers. Monetarists ought to welcome e-money, as a development that may help to bring a strict monetary base rule one step closer to perfection.

---

[4]Those who insist that this revenue is too small to be of great concern to the Treasury are invited to explain that agency's outspoken opposition to the plan— endorsed by the Federal Reserve—for payment of interest on bank reserve deposits.

14

ELECTRONIC MONEY AND MONETARY POLICY: SEPARATING FACT FROM FICTION

Bert Ely

Fundamentally, e-money is no different than all other forms of money in use today. Consequently, the monetary policy implications of e-money are nil. Hopefully, though, debating the implications of e-money will spark an overdue recasting of monetary theory to reflect present-day monetary realities rather than increasingly detrimental fictions (Ely 1996b). The new monetary theory should trigger the abandonment of interventionist monetary policy as we now know it, because the new theory will provide the basis for relying entirely on market forces to produce noninflationary economic growth and financial stability (Ely 1995).

Credit, Money, and E-Money

All forms of money that circulate in the United States today are forms of credit that also serve as media of exchange. In effect, money is merely a subset of credit. For example, currency is a credit instrument because it is a liability of its issuer, the federal government. Technically, a piece of currency is simply a small denomination, non-interest-bearing bearer bond of no fixed maturity that governments issue for just one reason—it provides interest-free debt financing. For example, in April 1996, currency financed 10.7 percent of the federal debt held by the public. As a credit instrument, currency serves as a store of value for its owner; as a medium of exchange, it facilitates transactions. Specie (i.e., gold and silver coins) is the only form of money that is not a form of credit, but such coins no longer circulate in market economies.

Bert Ely is President of Ely & Company, Inc.

Checkable bank deposits also are a form of credit—they are liabilities of a bank—as well as a medium of exchange. Unlike currency, though, checking account balances, as well as noncheckable deposits, finance bank assets (principally loans and investments). Travelers checks, such as those issued by American Express, likewise are credit instruments that are used to finance the issuer's assets. Debit cards, per se, are not money; instead, they are "keys" that provide electronic access to checkable bank deposits. Therefore, they can be used to issue what effectively are electronic checks (technically "value transfer instruments") that *transfer* deposits from payer to payee.

E-money, which is the money balance recorded electronically on a "stored-value" card, also is credit, for the balance on the card is a liability of its issuer. As with a depository institution, the card issuer uses funds paid by the card holder to acquire assets. The legal evidence of the issuer's liability to the cardholder consists of electronic bits and bytes recorded on the card. Similarly, the legal evidence of a government's liability to a currency holder is the piece of currency itself. For deposits, though, liability is evidenced by the records of the depository institution. For a long time, that liability was recorded on paper ledger cards; today, it almost always is accounted for in a computer.

Limits on the Growth of E-Money

The potential for fraud will greatly constrain the growth of e-money. That is, issuers of stored-value cards will have to hold electronic counterfeiting to a very low level if they wish to make money as card issuers. Just as retailers fight a never-ending war against shoplifting, issuers of stored-value cards must continually try to outsmart computer hackers attempting to increase the money balance on their stored-value cards.

Given the frequency with which hackers penetrate supposedly secure computer networks, issuers of stored-value cards will have to wage a constant battle to protect themselves against losses from fraud. Worse, they will not be able to respond quickly to a subversion of security measures (such as encryption algorithms) built into stored-value cards due to the time and expense that it will take to replace the compromised cards.

A recent incident in Japan illustrates the potential enormity of this fraud risk. In May 1996, subsidiaries of two large Japanese corporations (Mitsubishi and Sumitomo) reported a $585 million (63 billion yen) loss from the issuance of counterfeit stored-value cards used to purchase pachinko balls in pachinko parlors. Pachinko is a form of pinball on which players can gamble on the outcome. This loss occurred despite the fact that the pachinko cards had three levels of protection, including encryption. These cards, which were supposed to be highly secure, were compromised on a widescale basis—between January 1995 and April 1996, 1,400 people were arrested for making, using, or selling counterfeit pachinko cards (Pollack 1996).

Presumably, specific transactions could be recorded on stored-value cards (for example, $14.32 was transferred from card X to card Y or to merchant Z), which would create an audit trail by which the card issuer could determine who picked its pocket, when, and for how much. Audit trails, however, cool quickly when money is moving rapidly through international commerce, which supposedly is one of the attractions of e-money. Consequently, issuers of stored-value cards can protect themselves against fraud only if transactions data is transferred frequently from the card to the card issuer's computer. In that case, though, the card essentially becomes a debit card, merely activating the transfer of a deposit on the issuer's books from one party to another.

Holders of stored-value cards will be reluctant to carry large balances on their cards because of the loss they will suffer if they lose their card or the balance on it is erased. Hence, while consumers will use stored-value cards increasingly to pay for small purchases, currency will still be preferred for large or illicit purchases and in situations where currency is now held for store-of-value rather than transaction purposes. For example, it will be much safer to hide ten $100 bills in several locations rather than carry a $1,000 balance on a stored-value card used frequently to make small purchases.

Because of fraud and lost card problems, the aggregate amount of credit supplied by card users to card issuers will not be enormous. For example, if half the U.S. population over the age of 14 carried a stored-value card, 100 million cards would be in use today. Assuming an average balance on these cards of $100, the liability recorded on them would total $10 billion. That amount equals just 2.5 percent of the total amount of U.S. currency in circulation or 5 to 8 percent of currency circulating inside the United States.[1] These figures suggest that electronic money will not materially reduce the quantity of currency in circulation unless the velocity or turnover rate for e-money is much greater than it is for currency that is held for transaction purposes.

These figures also raise questions about the potential profitability of stored-value cards. Invested at a 6 percent yield, an average balance of $100 on a stored-value card would generate $6 annually of income for its issuer. Given the cost of marketing and providing cards and card readers, telecommunication and computer expenses, as well as fraud losses, issuers of stored-value cards may have to charge relatively high transaction fees that will discourage card use for the small transactions for which stored-value cards are best suited.

Monetary Policy Implications of E-Money

The monetary policy implications of stored-value cards are nil, with one slight exception—these cards reduce the federal government's "seigniorage" income, which is the interest expense that it saves by issuing currency. For example, a $10 billion shift in credit from government-issued currency to privately issued stored-value cards would cost the federal government about $600 million annually in seigniorage income ($10 billion times 6 percent, the approximate average cost of federal debt being issued today). Consequently, the government's annual budget deficit would increase by $600 million because it would have to issue an additional $10 billion in interest-bearing debt.

The government could recapture some of that lost income by treating the balances outstanding on stored-value cards as the equivalent of reservable deposits, which would then subject card balances to a "reserve requirement." Reservable deposits are balances in checkable bank accounts other than accounts classified as money market deposit accounts. Currently, commercial banks, thrift institutions, and credit unions meet their reserve requirement by holding reserves equal to 3 percent of the first $52 million of their reservable deposits plus 10 percent of reservable deposits over that amount.

---

[1]According to estimates by two Federal Reserve economists (Porter and Judson 1996), 55 to 70 percent of U.S. currency circulates *outside* the United States.

Depository institutions hold two forms of reserves—currency on hand (called vault cash) and non-interest-bearing deposits maintained at the Fed.

As Figure 1 illustrates, reserve requirements force owners of reservable deposits to make interest-free loans to the federal government that pass through depository institutions and then the Fed. In fact, reserve requirements are a tax on reservable deposits equal to the interest rate at which the depository institution could invest the funds on a short-term, low-risk basis. Assuming that depository institutions would reduce their reserves by $25 billion if reserve requirements were abolished, this tax costs these institutions, or rather their depositors, about $1.5 billion annually, assuming a 6 percent interest rate.

Taxing stored-value cards by subjecting them to reserve requirements would impede their use because this tax would reduce their profitability to card issuers. Therefore, unless Congress wants to curtail the use of stored-value cards by taxing them with reserve requirements, increased usage of such cards will add only slightly to the budget deficit.

E-money has no other monetary policy implications because U.S. monetary policy today consists entirely of the Fed's interest rate "signaling," which is discussed below. Contrary to widely held belief, the Fed does *not* control the money supply, for two reasons. First, the Fed, acting on behalf of the U.S. Treasury, passively supplies whatever quantities of currency that people voluntarily want to hold. This passivity exists because the federal government no longer can force currency into circulation since it does not pay its bills and other obligations in currency. In effect, the government cannot trigger a currency-driven inflation today by cranking up its printing presses and forcing billions of dollars of unwanted currency into circulation. Instead of being forced or pushed into circulation, U.S. currency today is *pulled* into circulation as banks turn worn currency into the Fed for replacement with freshly printed currency.

Second, the Fed passively supplies to the banking system whatever reserves depository institutions need to meet their reserve requirement so that it can control the quantity of "excess reserves" in the banking system. Excess reserves are those reserves on deposit at the Fed that exceed the required amount of reserves that depository institutions must hold. In effect, Fed-controlled excess reserves float

FIGURE 1
RESERVE REQUIREMENTS ARE A TAX ON RESERVABLE DEPOSITS

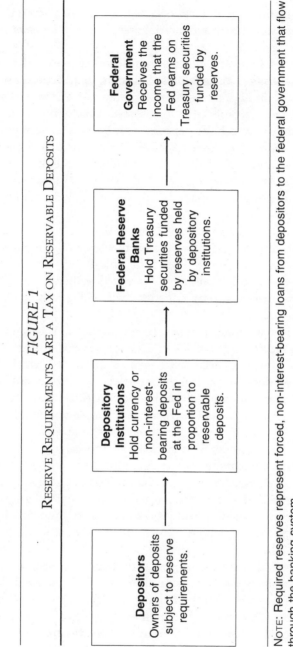

Depositors
Owners of deposits subject to reserve requirements.

Depository Institutions
Hold currency or non-interest-bearing deposits at the Fed in proportion to reservable deposits.

Federal Reserve Banks
Hold Treasury securities funded by reserves held by depository institutions.

Federal Government
Receives the income that the Fed earns on Treasury securities funded by reserves.

NOTE: Required reserves represent forced, non-interest-bearing loans from depositors to the federal government that flow through the banking system.

on top of a market-determined quantity of required reserves. Hence, reserve requirements do not constrain the growth of reservable deposits, the other component of the money supply.

If depository institutions increase the quantity of reservable deposits in the course of their lending activities or depositors decide to hold higher balances in accounts subject to reserve requirements, the Fed automatically supplies the additional reserves demanded by that deposit growth (Federal Reserve Bank of New York *Annual Report* for 1995: 17). Interestingly, required reserves have been dropping because banks increasingly use "sweep accounts" to automatically transfer customer deposits from reservable to nonreservable accounts, sometimes as frequently as daily. Sweep accounts probably account for much of the 13 percent, or $8 billion, drop in required reserves from December 1993 to March 1996. Total domestic deposits in depository institutions rose 4.6 percent during that period.

This shrinkage in required reserves reinforces the reality that the reservable deposit portion of the money supply, like the currency portion, is entirely demand-driven. Therefore, treating balances on stored-value cards as deposits will have no monetary policy implications because these balances will simply be another demand-driven component of a money supply that the Fed does not attempt to control. Attempting to control the money supply would conflict with the Fed's rate-signaling activities discussed below.

As an aside, because the Fed supplies whatever reserves the banking system needs, reserve requirements on deposits (which are liabilities of banks) no longer limit, if they ever did, the quantity of bank loans (which are assets of banks). Additionally, because reservable deposits now account for just 23 percent of all deposits, depository institutions today fund most of their loans and investments with nonreservable deposits and other funding sources whose quantity cannot be controlled by reserve requirements.

The Fed Funds Market

All depository institutions have to meet their reserve requirement over successive biweekly "reserve maintenance periods" that end on alternating Wednesdays, called "settlement Wednesdays." However, reserves are not spread proportionally over the banking system. Consequently, a "Fed Funds" market has emerged in which depository institutions lend reserves to one another, usually on an overnight and unsecured basis. Specifically, institutions with more reserves on deposit at the Fed than they need to meet their own reserve requirement (mostly smaller banks) lend or "sell" their excess reserves to other institutions (generally larger banks) who borrow or "buy" whatever reserves they need to meet their biweekly reserve requirement. The interest rate that lenders charge on Fed Funds loans is called the daily "Fed Funds" rate.

The Fed lubricates the Fed Funds market with the excess reserves, called systemwide excess reserves, that were mentioned above. For example, on a given day, institutions with excess reserves might hold total excess reserves of $100 billion while the remaining depository institutions might have a $99 billion reserve shortfall. The differential between these two amounts represents systemwide excess reserves of $1 billion, which happens to be the average amount of systemwide excess reserves in recent years. On some settlement Wednesdays, though, the Fed must increase excess reserves, by buying several billion dollars of its Treasury securities, to ensure that every depository institution can borrow sufficient reserves in the Fed Funds market to meet its biweekly reserve requirement.

Monetary Policy Today: Rate Signaling

Banks incur substantial operating expenses in complying with their reserve requirement as does the Fed in administering it. It would be far more efficient for all concerned if the government would simply levy an explicit tax on reservable deposits, although the desirability of any tax on bank deposits (essentially a wealth tax) is highly questionable. However inefficient the Fed Funds market may be, the Fed needs it so that it can use the daily Fed Funds rate to reinforce interest rate signals the Fed's Federal Open Market Committee (FOMC) periodically sends to the financial markets.

Specifically, eight times a year, the FOMC announces a Fed Funds Rate Target (FFRT). In effect, Fed bureaucrats tell the financial markets what they, the bureaucrats, believe should be the benchmark rate from which all other short-term interest rates should be set. Through its open market operations, the Fed reinforces the "announcement effect" of the FFRT on interest rates by manipulating the quantity of systemwide excess reserves to hold the daily Fed Funds interest rate close to the FFRT. Hence, the highly artificial Fed Funds market does double duty—banks are forced to use it to effectively pay a tax on their reservable deposits and it is a key component of the Fed's interest rate signaling activities.

Open market operations consist of the Fed buying and selling Treasury securities it owns that are financed by currency and reserves on deposit at the Fed. However, average systemwide excess reserves of $1 billion represent just a sliver—one-fourth of 1 percent—of the Fed's total liabilities. By manipulating the quantity of systemwide excess reserves, the Fed can, within limits, control the daily Fed Funds rate; on some days, though, particularly on settlement Wednesdays, the daily Fed Funds rate deviates significantly from the FFRT, sometimes by a full percentage point.

Interestingly, except for the daily Fed Funds rate, the Fed cannot move interest rates by the buying or selling of large quantities of Treasury securities through its open market operations. This is the case because transactions that move the daily Fed Funds rate are far too small to move rates in the market for short-term tradeable debt, which is approximately 2,000 times larger than the quantity of systemwide excess reserves. Unfortunately, many financial market participants still believe that the Fed can move interest rates other than the Fed Funds rate because they do not understand how interest rates are determined today. In fact, the Fed's influence over interest rates stems entirely from the mistaken *perception* that it can move rates, much as the Wizard of Oz's influence over the Munchkins grew from their belief in his power. Toto, though, revealed the truth (Ely 1996a).

Why The Fed Cannot Move Interest Rates

Any attempt by the Fed to move interest rates generally by buying or selling massive quantities of Treasury securities would quickly backfire on the Fed. For example, because Fed purchases of Treasuries increase systemwide excess reserves by a like amount, its additional purchase of even a few hundred million dollars of Treasuries would drive the daily Fed Funds rate from approximately its FFRT target to almost zero. Likewise, substantial Fed sales of Treasuries, which would reduce systemwide excess reserves, would drive the daily Fed Funds rate to the heavens. A large enough sale ($1 billion on average) could create *negative* systemwide reserves.

Interestingly, if the Fed's securities sales drove systemwide excess reserves into a negative position, the Fed would have to lend funds, through its "discount window," to the banking system so that every bank could meet its reserve requirement. These loans would have to be large enough to bring systemwide excess reserves back to at least zero. The net effect of the Fed's selling and then lending would merely shift the financing of just several billion dollars of a $3.6 trillion federal debt from the banking system to the capital markets while altering only slightly the mix of the government's net interest-bearing and non-interest-bearing debt. However, this shift would not alter the *net* amount of federal debt outstanding; only government revenues and spending can change a government's net debt level. This balance sheet tinkering by the Fed should not affect interest rates generally because it should not affect the expectations on which borrowers and lenders set interest rates. These expectations include the future real rate of interest, the future inflation rate, and credit risks.

While the Fed's interest-rate signaling should not affect interest rate expectations, the Fed was able, through its signaling, to cause a near doubling of short-term rates between February 1994 and February 1995. The Fed's impact occurred only because the financial markets had been snookered by the Fed in 1992 and 1993 into bringing short-term rates too low, which created an excessively steep yield curve that fostered a speculative bubble in the stock and bond markets that burst in 1994 when the Fed finally signaled that it was time for rates to rise. In effect, the financial markets, in a decidedly unmarket-like response, subordinated their own expectations about the future to the expectations of the financial markets' central planner, the Federal Reserve System.

The Fed would suffer two consequences if it did engineer a large gap between the FFRT and other interest rates that banks thought would last more than a few weeks. First, that gap would destroy the perception that the Fed can move interest rates, other than the daily Fed Funds rate. In effect, this gap would severely undermine the Fed's already declining influence over interest rates. In effect, a clear demonstration of the inability of the Fed's open market operations to force market rates to comply with the FFRT would destroy the FFRT's announcement effect.

Second, a large, prolonged gap would greatly shrink the size of the Fed Funds market as individual banks harmed by the gap (they receive a below-market rate on Fed Funds sold or pay an above-market rate on Fed Funds bought) would quickly align their actual reserves with their reserve requirement. For example, banks that usually sell Fed Funds would reduce their deposits and other liabilities, buy securities, and make loans to reduce their quantity of excess reserves.

The potentially stimulative effect of these banks expanding the amount of credit outstanding would merely offset, though, the contractionary actions of the banks that usually buy Fed Funds. The latter banks would increase their deposits, sell securities, and reduce their loans to eliminate their reserves shortfall. Once burnt by a large and persistent Fed Funds rate gap, depository institutions (both Fed Funds buyers and sellers) would then be slow to expose themselves again to the risk that the Fed would materially delink the Fed Funds rate from other short-term interest rates. In effect, the Fed Funds market exists today largely because the FFRT, and therefore the daily Fed Funds rate, does not deviate significantly from short-term, market-driven rates. A shriveled Fed Funds market would further undermine the import of the FFRT.

One interest rate that does track the FFRT is the prime rate that banks use as a benchmark in pricing many loans, such as small business, credit card, and home equity loans. In recent years, the prime rate has usually floated at 3 percent above the FFRT. The prime rate is not a true market rate, though, because it is not subject to the usual marketplace bargaining that drives minute-by-minute changes in other rates. If, however, a sustained gap developed between the FFRT and market interest rates, banks would no longer tie the prime rate to the FFRT. Instead, they would explicitly link the prime rate to market interest rates because banks have to pay a market rate of interest on the deposits and other borrowings that fund their loans and investments.

Markets Can Control Inflation Better than the Fed

Today's reality (versus perception) is that the Fed is impotent as a mover and shaker in the financial markets. All the Fed really can do is express its opinion about interest rates, which it does when the FOMC periodically announces its FFRT. The Fed focuses on interest rates, and not the money supply, because Fed bureaucrats understand that interest rates are the principal factor controlling credit growth. In fact, it would be impossible for the Fed to control both interest rates and credit growth; socialism collapsed because it is not possible for any central planner, even central banks, to control both the price and quantity of an economic good, which credit is.

The rate of credit growth is crucial because it is credit, not money, that finances economic activity, specifically the purchase of goods, services, and assets. Money is merely that portion of the credit supply that also serves as media of exchange. Inflation therefore is caused by excessively rapid credit growth; that is, purchasing power, boosted by rapid credit growth, grows faster than the supply of goods and services available for purchase. The old saying, too much money chasing too few goods causes inflation, should be restated to read: inflation occurs when too much *credit* chases too few goods.

The unspoken conceit underlying the Fed's interest rate signaling is that Fed bureaucrats are more qualified than the financial markets to price an economic good, specifically to hold credit growth to a noninflationary rate. That conceit is fallacious, though, as it is in all markets, since markets invariably can do a better job of pricing goods and services than a government central planning agency, which the Fed is. Further, it is in the financial markets' self-interest to set nominal interest rates that will produce noninflationary credit growth because of the clearly opposed interests of debtors and creditors (debtors like inflation; creditors like deflation). That is, the bargaining between debtors and creditors should produce nominal interest rates that will generate neither inflation nor deflation. Additionally, because participants in a market economy usually operate more efficiently in a noninflationary environment, there should be broad market, and therefore broad political, support for marketplace bargaining over interest rates that produces noninflationary credit growth.

The markets' tendency to follow the Fed's lead in setting short-term rates has two especially deleterious effects. First, because of the consensual nature of its decisionmaking, the FOMC tends to lag, often by months, in adjusting the FFRT to reflect changes in economic conditions that warrant changes in interest rates.

Second, because the FOMC meets only eight times a year, the FFRT is adjusted too infrequently. Short-term interest rates, like all other prices, should fluctuate daily to reflect ongoing shifts in the supply and demand for savings (which determines real interest rates), supply-side "inflation shocks" (which influence the inflation premium embedded in nominal interest rates), and other factors that affect rates. Consequently, over the short term, the Fed's attempt to use the FFRT to peg short-term interest rates creates too much rigidity at the short end of the interest rate yield curve. That is, short-term rates do not fluctuate enough over a period of weeks or a few months. This rigidity whipsaws long-term interest rates, and hence the real economy, because the financial markets incorporate in nominal long-term interest rates the Fed-induced mispricing of short-term rates that creates inflationary or deflationary credit demand. In effect, the Fed's supposed desire to stabilize interest rates actually is counterproductive.

Longer term, the Fed's rate-pegging accentuates and even creates the business cycle by pegging the short end of the yield curve too high or too low for sustained periods. Consequently, the yield curve is too shallow or too steep (as it was in 1993), which in turn overemphasizes interest-rate restraint at one end of the yield curve while simultaneously underemphasizing it, relatively speaking, at the other end of the curve. Fortunately, borrowers increasingly can neutralize the Fed's rate distortions by directly, or with hedging instruments, shifting the effective maturity of their borrowings so as to at least partially escape the impact of the Fed's rate-pegging.

U.S. inflation in recent decades has been caused by various government distortions of interest rates, including at times the Fed's signaling of excessively low interest rates that the financial markets have unwisely followed. Other causes of inflation have been interest tax subsidies, government credit guarantees, and mispriced deposit insurance.

The high inflation of the late 1970s and early 1980s was a product of extremely low and at times negative real interest rates that the Fed engineered in the late 1960s and the 1970s. However, the growing power of the financial markets, and perhaps of greater importance, the markets' growing awareness of their power, is rapidly undermining the ability of governments and their central banks to distort interest rates, which is why inflation has been declining throughout the world. Specifically, the financial markets have become more effective in neutralizing government distortions of interest rates. Getting the Fed out of the rate signaling business would further enhance the markets' effectiveness. Utilizing the cross-guarantee concept to privatize banking regulation and its attendant deposit insurance and systemic risks would eliminate the problem of mispriced government deposit insurance (Ely 1994, Petri and Ely 1995).

Conclusion

Hopefully, the debate over e-money and stored-value cards will spark a fundamental examination of present-day monetary realities that will replace fiction with fact, thereby creating the basis for a monetary theory that relies on market forces, and not on central banks, to produce noninflationary credit and economic growth. Hopefully, this paper has provided a solid framework for constructing that new theory.

References

Ely, B. (1994) "Financial Innovation and Deposit Insurance: The 100 Percent Cross-Guarantee Concept." *Cato Journal* 13(3): 413–36.

Ely, B. (1995) "Is Monetary Policy Needed?" *The Banker* (London) (October): 14–5.

Ely, B. (1996a) "A Hard Look at Fed's Wizard of Oz." *American Banker*, 15 February: 18.

Ely, B. (1996b) "Does Money Count? Findings of Fact About Present-Day U.S. Monetary Realities." Mimeo. Ely & Company, Inc., Alexandria, Va.

Petri, T., and Ely, B. (1995) "Better Banking for America: The 100 Percent Cross-Guarantee Concept." *Common Sense* (Fall): 96–112.

Pollack, A. (1996) "Counterfeiters of a New Stripe Give Japan One More Worry." *New York Times*, 20 June: D1.

Porter, R.D., and Judson, R.A. (1996) "The Location of U.S. Currency: How Much Is Abroad?" *Federal Reserve Bulletin* 82 (October): 883–903.

15

MONEY IN THE 21ST CENTURY

Jerry L. Jordan and Edward J. Stevens

Innovation in money is nothing new. For centuries, the fundamental forces of technological innovation and market competition have been altering both the forms in which money is held and the methods by which its ownership is transferred.

What *is* new in the present dialogue are the technologies used to make payments, and their names, such as cybercash, e-cash, and smart cards.

What is *not* new are economists' underlying concepts and theoretical framework for thinking about monetary policy. Goods and services are what we use to satisfy our wants. Money prices are what we use to state the values of goods and services. The mission of monetary policy is to maintain stable purchasing power, avoiding both deflationary excess demands for money and inflationary excess supplies of money.

What we need to *change* in the emerging dialogue is our use of conventional terms that have been only temporarily meaningful in the 20th century, such as "deposit" and "commercial bank." A growing segment of the public can see no real distinction between a deposit and either a mutual fund share or a transferable, interest-bearing credit balance. Similarly, the statutory distinction between a financial firm chartered as a commercial bank and another financial firm that offers many of the same services, but does not have a bank charter, is not important.

Looking out over the next century, it is not possible to predict how fast things will change, and exactly what forms innovations will take. Indeed, much uncertainty remains about the central bank

Jerry L. Jordan is President and Chief Executive Officer of the Federal Reserve Bank of Cleveland. Edward J. Stevens is a consultant and economist at the Bank.

implications of potential changes in monetary mechanisms. Three points:

- Money innovations in the past have tended to reduce the demand for central bank money, but the reliability of monetary policy depends not so much on the amount demanded as on the predictability of that amount. Innovations probably will reduce demand for central bank money even further in the 21st century, but it is much too soon to say whether the predictability of that demand, and therefore the potential reliability of monetary policy, will be reduced in any significant way.
- Some analysts contend that holdings of central bank money (currency and deposits at the Reserve Banks) will virtually disappear in the next century—just as holdings of commodity money have done in the 20th century. Nevertheless, monetary authorities will still determine the price level as long as final settlement of tax and other obligations takes place using central bank liabilities.
- Whether the declining demand for central bank money might influence the role of national currencies as primary standards of value is not yet known. We are encouraged, however, that both theoretical and empirical economic research are focusing energies on this topic. The possibility of a stable, privately issued currency that is not convertible into a national currency is the subject of a growing literature.

After a brief overview of innovations in money regimes, we elaborate on each of these points.

Innovations in Money Regimes

Our view is that people choose to use as "money" those devices that economize best on the use of other real resources in gathering information and conducting transactions, and that high-confidence moneys drive low-confidence moneys out of common usage. Monetary history records repeated innovations in the assets that have been readily transferable stores of value, and in the mechanisms used for transferring those asset values. As recently as the 19th century, "money" meant both the money storage asset and the money transfer mechanism. Full-bodied commodity money, fractional coin, government fiat currency, and bank notes all provided assets for storing value and, at the same time, vehicles for instantaneous, face-to-face transfers of value, with finality.

The inconvenience of making face-to-face payments in an increasingly integrated national economy was avoided by accepting the cost and risk of delayed payment finality. Local clearinghouses became part of the transfer technology, facilitating both the clearing and settlement of checks drawn on asset values stored in local bank deposits. At greater distances, payers could purchase "exchange," consisting of a local bank's check drawn on its distant correspondent, which could then be mailed to the payee, bringing the post office into the transfer mechanism. The U.S. Post Office, as well as some commercial enterprises like American Express, operated independent paper money-order services for transferring money values over distances, while Western Union did the same thing by telegraph.

In the first decades of this century, telegraphic transfers of balances for same-day value were the cutting edge of money technology. The dominant retail money technology was still shifting to paper checks drawn on commercial bank demand deposits. Over the past several decades, rapidly declining costs of computing and telecommunications have allowed a wider variety of assets to be exchanged very quickly, fulfilling some of the "store of value" functions of money, but these assets are only indirectly capable of being transferred to third parties.

Successively broader definitions of money in the United States have recorded the widening field of effectively monetized assets. As we come to the end of the century, M2 includes NOW account and money market deposit account balances at banks and nonbank depository institutions; shares held in money market mutual funds; plus the original combination of currency, demand deposits, and small time and savings deposits. This certainly commingles "dollars" and assets denominated in dollars. Moreover, value held in all these assets can be transferred directly to third parties by paper or electronic payment orders, or, at least, moved so rapidly from one kind of account to another as to be indistinguishable from a direct third-party transfer.

The increasing speed of transactions has been a critical part of the innovation process. At the cutting edge of money technology, corporate America is moving beyond batch processing and air couriers, to networks for integrated accounting and payments processing systems. The definition of an instantaneous money transfer—not by check, but by ATM or direct computer connection—is moving inexorably toward "real time," on a par with exchanges of currency, but without the need to be physically face-to-face. And the closer technology brings us to real-time *remote* payments, the closer we are to genuine 24-hour banking and trading, and a worldwide set of assets that might be used for wealth storage, at least for those who are willing to accept some currency risk.

The proliferation of money assets and increasing speed of money transfers are two trends that clearly will persist into the next century. So, too, will a third trend—the elimination of regulatory and other legal restrictions on the money industry erected by governments. On a global scale, modern communications technology ensured the free flow of information through the Iron Curtain, and flattened the Berlin Wall. In the United States, that same technology has flattened artificial walls between groups of depository and other regulated financial institutions, and between regulated and unregulated institutions. Telecommunications-based information technology has made it ever cheaper to avoid costly regulations. Initially, this perpetuated a kind of cat-and-mouse game between regulators and markets. In banking, at least, that game now is ending. For example, last year brought the advent of accounting programs that sweep reservable deposits temporarily into nonreservable form for all the retail deposits of a bank, not just its corporate cash management customers. As a result, the average reserve requirement tax rate is becoming ineffective at a vast majority of depository institutions.

The rapid spread and ultimate success of sweep programs epitomizes 50 years of experience with erecting and flattening arbitrary regulatory walls between industries. In the long run, those walls won't stand. Regulation created profit incentives for banks to avoid reserve requirement and deposit rate ceilings and line-of-business restrictions by taking their money business outside the traditional orbit of the banking industry, lest it be taken there by nonbanks. The same restrictions created incentives for banks' competitors to bring the business of banking into the orbit of nonbanking industries. Sometimes the banks prevailed; sometimes nonbanks prevailed. Never did the regulators prevail, and the walls have come tumbling down. Regardless of whether Congress ever removes Glass–Steagall restrictions, the long-run futility of using regulations to enforce arbitrary restrictions seems well documented.

Past Innovations and the Demand for Central Bank Money

Descriptions of smart card and Internet moneys suggest that developers of electronic moneys might be nonfinancial organizations that build on foundations already laid by their existing, unique product lines. A subway system might move from a stored-value fare card toward a more general-purpose stored-value card. A long-distance carrier might build on its nationwide commercial and consumer network.

The predicted impact of such innovations on the central bank has a familiar ring. Around the turn of the century, as the use of checking accounts became widespread, analysts recognized that these deposits were substitutes for traditional gold and paper money. To account for the effect of this substitution on what we now call monetary policy, discussion focused on the resulting increase in the level of national income relative to the quantity of what was the equivalent of today's central bank money. Then, in the 1950s, the thrift industry enjoyed overwhelming competitive success in providing assets that were so liquid as to be close substitutes for checking account deposits at commercial banks. Experts recognized that the ratio of national income to a noninflationary supply of central bank money increased when thrifts issued monetary assets without holding significant reserves of central bank money. In the 1970s, discussion focused on electronic funds transfer systems. Once again, the concern was about increases in the ratio of national income to a noninflationary supply of central bank money resulting from reduced needs for inventories of money. Electronics was expected to allow existing moneys to be transferred with greater speed and precision over emerging telecommunications networks that would link merchants and customers and banks.

Innovations in monetary assets and transfer systems complicate monetary policy decisionmaking by producing short-run changes in the quantity of central bank money that would be consistent with stable purchasing power. Monetary targets are more difficult to define and achieve during the transition from one type of money regime to another. But a smaller demand for central bank money does not, by itself, make it forever more difficult to maintain financial stability. The issue is whether there can be offsetting increases in the precision with which the central bank can control the supply of its monetary liabilities. We are not aware of anyone who suggests that the long-run decrease in the demand for the monetary base relative to the nominal level of national income has led the Federal Reserve seriously astray, allowing the purchasing power of the dollar to fluctuate as much as it has in the 20th century or to decline as much as it has in the postwar period. However rough, the policy process can still operate through feedback directly from movements in the observed price level.

Checking the facts against the expectation of reduced demand for central bank money is instructive. Despite all the new types of monetary assets and transfers, the average annual growth rate of the monetary base has been only about 1.5 percentage points slower than the growth rate of nominal GDP since 1959, when the current monetary data series began. The deposit (reserve) component of the base has been growing 4 percentage points slower than nominal GDP each year, on average, while currency has been growing at about the same rate as nominal GDP. These results are influenced, however, by outflows of U.S. currency to foreign markets that have needed a more reliable money than provided by their own central banks. If we assume that foreign holdings of dollar currency have gone from a negligible percentage of the total outstanding in 1959 to almost two-thirds today, then *domestically* held central bank money has been increasing at a rate 3 percentage points slower than nominal GDP each year over the last third of the century.

Future Innovations and the Demand for Central Bank Money

Looking ahead to the 21st century, we can expect continued reductions in the demand for central bank money. Substitutes for, and economizers of, current money assets, and increasingly sophisticated money transfer systems, all are on the horizon.

But will this just be a case of "déjà vu all over again," another episode of innovation shifting the demand for central bank money, making short-run mischief with quantitative monetary targets? Perhaps not, for another possibility must be recognized. The kernel of the money question emerging on the 21st century horizon is not just about further reductions in demand for central bank money, or even instability induced by more unpredictable demand. Rather, what may be new and different about the 21st century is the possibility that central bank money might virtually disappear—that is, some have posed the theoretical possibility that, in the limit, there will be no appreciable domestic demand at all for central bank money—whether currency or banks' balances at Reserve Banks.

Discussions of smart card and Internet moneys hint at this radically new monetary future with little place for high-powered base money issued by the central bank. One focus is on the degree to which value embedded in smart card memories will be the liability of commercial firms or of financial institutions, and whether traditional regulations such as reserve requirements and capital ratios might extend to smart cards. These questions, while important in the short run, may be largely beside the point in the long run. Reserve requirements already are becoming a dead issue, killed by technology and competition. Capital ratio requirements are meeting the same fate, from the same forces. To the extent capital ratios might be made more onerous than the value of the safety net services they buy, they are unlikely to survive in the long run. Thus, regulation of new electronic moneys is unlikely to create a demand for central bank money.

Smart card and Internet moneys must meet quality control standards in some form, of course, either from safety net supervision or from pressures of customers and competitors in the market. Safety and soundness will always be relevant to customers' choices among moneys. Similarly, the relative quantities of these moneys will be controlled by their success in competing with alternative monetary assets and transfer mechanisms like credit cards and debit cards, as well as paper checks and electronic transfers of account balances.

Issuance of successful electronic moneys by the central bank itself would ensure a continuing demand for central bank liabilities. The object would be to allow electronic payments with the finality of paper currency, but with the divisibility, security, and ease of transportation associated with the new electronic devices. This possibility should not be ruled out. For now, however, neither government regulation of private issuers nor direct government issuance of electronic forms of currency seems likely to ensure significant demand for central bank money over the next century.

Today, complete substitution of electronic moneys for currency in domestic use would still leave a substantial quantity of central bank money outstanding. Foreign holdings, remember, are estimated to represent about two-thirds of the value of U.S. currency now outstanding. The durability of this demand may depend more on the relative qualities of U.S. and foreign monetary management in the next century than on the relative costs and features of currency and its electronic substitutes. It is not at all clear, however, even if the United States were assured of another century of foreign demand for central bank money, that controlling the supply of currency to foreign holders would be effective in conducting domestic monetary policy.

Another hint of a radically new 21st century monetary future comes from looking at the demand for central bank money by depository institutions. If technology and competition were to eliminate demands for currency by the general public, then depository institutions' derived demand for vault cash also would wither. Moreover, technology, competition, and regulatory actions have already eliminated a substantial part of the demand for Reserve Bank balances to satisfy reserve requirements. This process could continue until virtually no bank in the United States was constrained by reserve requirement regulations as currently structured. Therefore, low reserve requirements may be just as untenable tomorrow as high requirements proved to be in the past.

Reserve requirements are not the only reason for maintaining an account balance with a Reserve Bank. Many depository institutions maintain clearing balances at Reserve Banks. One reason is to provide a cushion to protect against daylight and overnight overdrafts. Another is to earn a market-based rate of return, although it can be used only to pay for financial services provided by the Reserve Banks.

Neither reason for holding a clearing balance is a very robust source of demand for central bank money. Overdrafts can be avoided in other ways. One is to apply information technology to the sequencing of debits and credits during a day to minimize daylight overdrafts and avoid surprise debits at the end of a day. Another is to organize and participate in multilateral clearing and net settlement arrangements for money and securities transfers. Substituting these for Reserve Bank services could reduce the need for an overdraft cushion.

These and other alternatives to holding balances may not be especially attractive today because banks tend to use the Reserve Banks' priced payment services in sufficient volume to make earnings credits valuable. Over time, however, definitive paper instruments will lose market share, eventually rendering check and noncash collection services obsolete. Moreover, commercial competitors are likely to continue making inroads on the growing automated clearing house market that once was the almost exclusive domain of the Reserve Banks. Unless the Reserve Banks were to develop appealing new services, much of their bankers' banking seems vulnerable to technological obsolescence.

It is not really a complete flight of fancy to foresee central bank money becoming insignificant in the domestic economy. In time, the public may find commercially provided electronic money attractive as a replacement for currency. Reserve requirements are not likely to provide a solid floor under the demand for Reserve Bank money by depository institutions. Finally, demand for clearing balances at the Reserve Banks could decline as earnings credits become less valuable.

What Role Remains for the Central Bank?

Even with little demand by the public to hold central bank liabilities, central banks remain the only source of the national currency units that are required to settle domestic tax obligations. Furthermore, for the foreseeable future, final net settlement of imbalances between various competing, privately issued, electronic moneys will be in the form of central bank liabilities. The Federal Reserve, and every other central bank of which we are aware, provides settlement finality as a payments service. Final settlement represents an ultimate, official guarantee of values exchanged by Reserve Bank depositors and their customers. Finality may be rendered on a gross basis, as the Reserve Banks do in making immediate, irrevocable Fedwire transfers, or on a net basis, as the Reserve Banks do in settling the zero-sum end-of-day positions of depositors who belong to a multilateral clearing house arrangement like CHIPS.

Central banks effect settlement when they post irrevocable debits and offsetting credits to two or more depository institutions' account balances. In the United States, those account balances must be zero or positive at the end of each day, and typically total in the $30 billion range. At the Bank of England, in contrast, aggregate balances are close to zero at the end of each day. This highlights the fact that *overnight* balances are not necessary, either in the aggregate or for an individual depository institution, as long as the supply of *intraday* balances is sufficient to accommodate mismatched flows of depositors' receipts and payments without payments gridlock. Intraday balances might come from central bank intraday credit, as in real-time gross settlement systems like Fedwire. Alternatively, participants in payments networks like CHIPS might supply intraday credit to one another, economizing on the need for central bank balances by delaying finality until one or more net settlements during the day.

Looked at in this way, the settlement function of the central bank could continue even if holding central bank money overnight were no longer a widespread practice. Central bank money may not be used as an asset in which to store value overnight and longer, but still could be critical as a vehicle for transferring value during a day.

The monetary policy function of the central bank—maintaining constant purchasing power of the standard of value, or unit of account—still must be fulfilled even if central bank deposit liabilities denominated in the national currency unit enjoy only a fleeting existence during the course of each day. The long-run equilibrium value of the domestic demand for monetary base could approach zero as it is now measured, at the close of business each day. The policy authority, however, could still control the terms on which payments system institutions would acquire balances needed to make payments during the day. It could also control the terms on which institutions would rid themselves of excess balances accumulated during the day, in order to return to a zero balance at the close of business. Treasury and central bank payments and receipts, at least, would be critical factors in determining whether depositories developed an aggregate net debit or net credit position at any moment during a day, just as is the case today. The mechanisms a central bank might find useful in controlling the intraday supply of its liabilities to the private sector, of course, might be quite different from those now used to maintain more than $400 billion in overnight liabilities, but the principle involved—zero excess supply and demand at a desired level of a money market interest rate—would seem to be essentially the same.

We have just illustrated how the settlement and monetary policy roles of the central bank might be carried on in the next century, even in the absence of a conventional demand for central bank money. "Might be carried on" is different, of course, from "will be carried on," and we confess to uncertainty about the impacts of less-readily analyzed pressures for change that might accompany declining demand for central bank money.

Conclusion

We can foresee the possibility of only fleeting daily demands for central bank money in the 21st century, but we can neither predict that outcome, nor forecast its consequences on payments settlement methods and mechanisms for managing the purchasing power of the unit of account. Our uncertainty is relieved, however, by seeing one direction in which academic research has been moving. The general topic of "free banking" can be thought of as dealing with how an economic and financial system would operate in the absence of state interventions such as a central bank. Alternative definitions of "free banking" are being used, it's true, ranging from a money industry in which banks operate without reference to a common unit of account, to a money industry not much different from the long-run situation we have been assuming, in which financial markets avoid all regulations that provide no quid pro quo. Nonetheless, research evolving in these directions is precisely what is needed for the next century, when there is a good chance that central bank money will not be in much demand.

16

THE EFFECTS OF E-MONEY ON MONETARY POLICY: COMMENTS ON SELGIN, ELY, AND JORDAN/STEVENS

William A. Niskanen

It is remarkable that three thoughtful analyses of the effects of e-money on monetary policy come to three very different conclusions.

Selgin's Analysis

Let me first address the paper by George Selgin, because this paper makes the simplest point. Selgin concludes that the substitution of e-money for currency will *increase* the effectiveness of monetary policy by reducing the variance in the money multiplier due to changes in the public demand for currency. The import of Selgin's conclusion, I suggest, is dependent on two assumptions: (1) the availability of e-money will substantially reduce the demand for currency, and (2) monetary policy is best conducted by controlling some monetary aggregate for which the central bank can be held responsible.

I doubt whether Selgin's first assumption, that e-money will crowd out much currency, is a probable outcome, but I must acknowledge that I do not understand the current demand for currency. Even if only one-third of U.S. currency is in circulation in this country, that amount is about $500 per person or $1,000 per member of the labor force. I have no idea who holds all this currency and where. I doubt whether the average amount held in one's wallet is more than $50. If e-money replaces all wallet currency that would only reduce the demand for currency by up to 10 percent. If that is the only effect, there would be no substantial change in the level and variance of the money multiplier.

William A. Niskanen is Chairman of the Cato Institute.

On the issue of how best to conduct monetary policy, I suggest that the jury is still out. Given the variance of both the income velocity of money and the money multiplier, the central bank may do better to directly target some economic aggregate, such as nominal GDP or the price level, and make whatever adjustments in their monetary instruments are necessary to stay on the target path. My own contribution to this debate is to recommend that the most appropriate target path is the nominal level of domestic final sales. In some sense, this debate involves a tradeoff between economic importance and institutional accountability. On this issue, I suggest, it is better to roughly control some important economic aggregate than to precisely control some monetary aggregate—better to be roughly right than precisely wrong. For a central bank that uses such a recursive, error-correcting monetary policy, a reduction of the variance of the money multiplier is not very important.

Ely's Analysis

The paper by Bert Ely, in contrast, concludes that the substitution of e-money for currency will have no effect on monetary policy. Ely offers two quite different arguments for this conclusion.

First, he focuses a jeweler's eye on the commercial prospects for e-money. He suggests that the market for stored-value cards may be no larger than about $10 billion and questions whether the gross income of about $600 million would be sufficient to cover the costs of providing and marketing these cards. In this case, there would be no significant effect on the demand for currency. On this issue, I suspect that Ely is probably right, although his estimate of the potential market for stored-value cards may be off by a factor of 2 in either direction.

Second, he uses his paper to summarize his broader challenge to the conventional perspective on monetary policy. He asserts that the Federal Reserve does not control the money supply because it cannot; both currency and bank reserves, he contends, are demand determined with the federal government passively supplying whatever the market demands. Moreover, he asserts that the Federal Reserve's only effect on interest rates is a consequence of a broad but false perception that they can actually change rates.

On this issue, I am reminded of my mother's comment when I marched in the high school band that "Everyone is out of step but my Billy." On this issue, in other words, I suggest that Ely is wrong. Bert and I have talked about this issue several times, but he has yet to persuade me by the internal logic of his analysis or to pose a testable statement that could be checked against the evidence. I am especially skeptical of his assertion that everyone other than Bert Ely is fooled about the ability of the Federal Reserve to change interest rates. But I invite you to make your own judgment on this issue.

Jordan and Stevens's Analysis

For balance, Jerry Jordan and Edward Stevens play the role of the typical two-handed economist. On the one hand, they argue, several trends are apparent and will continue:

- Technology and market developments will continue to reduce the demand for currency and bank reserves, possibly to zero.
- These same developments will reduce the ability of governments to regulate the money industry.

On the other hand, they argue, the magnitudes of these effects are uncertain and, maybe, cannot be anticipated with any confidence.

On both of these issues, I suggest, Jordan and Stevens are well informed, thoughtful, probably correct, and not very helpful. The issue is not our inability to forecast the effects of technological and institutional innovation. I had hoped, however, for some advice on how the various affected institutions may best respond to the current and sequentially developing information about the effects of these innovations. We may be on the eve of a revolution on the nature of money and banking, but what should individuals, business managers, private bankers, government regulators, and central bankers do about this, if anything, when they go to work tomorrow morning?

Conclusion

My view is that the three papers provide little guidance about the effects of e-money on monetary policy, other than to suggest that the possible effects may range from trivial to revolutionary. In my judgment, the specific effects of e-money will be small; I do not expect stored-value cards to substitute for much currency, banks have a strong incentive to reduce their reserves whatever the developments in technology, and the effects of many changes is just to reduce float. For this observer, the regulatory implications of e-money seen more interesting and more important.

PART IV

THE FUTURE OF BANKING

17

CREATING AN ELECTRONIC MONETARY SYSTEM

Sholom Rosen

The Electronic Monetary System (EMS) is a highly versatile and highly secure payment system that creates, secures, and exchanges electronic notes in multiple currencies. EMS is a serious attempt to build a comprehensive electronic money system that reflects the interests of the regulatory authorities, the banking system as it exists today, and the rapid manner in which technology will continue to change. The system is the first to support, in a secure fashion, electronic cash payments for both retail and wholesale customers.

Having worked to develop EMS since 1991, Citibank was awarded two important technology patents covering EMS and electronic money in 1995 by the U.S. Patent and Trademark Office. The bank also has several other patents pending in the area of electronic commerce.

Implications of Electronic Money

The implications of electronic money in today's globally networked world are enormous. The steadily growing popularity of PCs, the Internet, on-line services, and electronic gadgets of every kind means more and more individuals are benefiting from technology's push into the consumer world. Electronic money introduces an entirely new scheme for transacting business. Consumers and merchants will be able to perform fairly complicated financial transactions without having to go to a bank.

Sholom Rosen is Vice President and Head of Emerging Technology at Citibank.

Operation of the EMS

EMS involves four basic types of participants:

1. *Issuing banks* generate electronic notes (money) on demand to customers; there can be any number from one to many.
2. *Correspondent banks* accept and distribute the electronic money.
3. *Clearing banks* clear issuing bank notes and settle accounts.
4. *Subscribers* (buyers and sellers) use Money Modules (essentially a secure processing environment) for storing their electronic money, performing online transactions with a bank, or exchanging electronic money with other Money Modules.

EMS notes can be created on demand in any currency. The notes can be withdrawn as cash from a DDA (Demand Deposit Account) or used to draw down an approved line of credit. Each note carries a complete electronic audit trail and is reconciled by the issuing bank. EMS cash notes circulate and can be redeemed at the bank or transferred to another subscriber. And like cash, the value of each note is guaranteed by a bank.

With the potential for fraudulent use of electronic money systems, EMS was designed to include the three basic principles of security: prevention, detection, and containment. EMS addresses prevention through the use of cryptographic protocols and physical protection of the Money Modules. Each communications session is authenticated and secured, and a Security Server authenticates each Money Module by periodically validating its electronic certificate. A special protective coating makes the Money Module hardware itself tamperproof, thus physically protecting the sensitive software contained within it.

To aid in identifying duplicate or counterfeit notes, EMS (invisibly to the user) regularly "sweeps" electronic notes into the bank for validation and control, and then returns new notes to the Money Module. The system also reconciles notes cleared to notes issued. EMS "contains" suspected fraudulent use in several ways: First, electronic notes carry an expiration date that limits the window of opportunity for transfers. (This does not cause the value of the notes to expire—just the ability to move them.) EMS can also block both the further use of Money Modules that are known to be corrupted and the further circulation of fraudulent notes. The system can also cause a Money Module certificate to expire, thereby putting the Money Module out of commission.

Establishing Trust

EMS strikes a balance between the needs for security and privacy. The system addresses the twin issues of system security and customer privacy in a manner that guarantees the traceability of every note without knowing the identity of the customer. Protecting the customers' trust and system integrity are critical.

EMS provides an infrastructure for applications such as simple retail point-of-sale, electronic payments between corporations, interbank payments, and party-to-party foreign exchange.

The technology also extends well beyond moving money securely. Additional technology addresses and resolves the security and processing needs required for commerce over open networks. The slow growth of electronic commerce over "open" networks, such as the Internet, is due not only to the poor security across the network but also the absence of adequate protection for the buyer and seller as they attempt to conduct business without any face-to-face contact.

One basic risk of doing business over open networks, for example, is that of "pulling the plug"—either the buyer can pull the plug upon receipt of the goods (but before paying) or the seller can pull the plug upon receipt of payment (but before shipping the goods). In cyberspace, the secure receipt of both payment and electronic goods must be redefined.

A companion technology known as Trusted Agent was designed along with EMS to guarantee payment and delivery for electronic goods and services purchased over the Internet or any open network. Through the use of secure transaction "umbrellas," EMS and Trusted Agent together can ensure that both the customer and the merchant are safe because payment and delivery are locked and synchronized. Payments will be released to the merchant, and the electronic goods released to the buyer, only upon the successful exchange of both sides of the transaction.

The combination of EMS and Trusted Agent for the first time enables truly open spontaneous electronic commerce because both the buyer and the seller are protected from the risks associated with not doing business face-to-face. Trusted Agent not only integrates information with the movement of money, but can verify that the cybermerchant is actually who it purports to be. Trusted Agent also carries information explaining the nature of a payment (such as an invoice number, which is required by businesses when posting payments), and creates and delivers a secure receipt at the end of a transaction.

Trusted Agent's ability to guarantee payment and delivery need not be restricted to electronic money applications. Trusted Agent in addition can deliver credit cards, or debit cards as the payment medium over an electronic network.

The versatility and security of the combination of EMS and Trusted Agent technologies can provide the needed functionality and trust of the physical marketplace to open networks.

18

THE FUTURE OF CURRENCY COMPETITION
Catherine England

Economists generally accept that competition in supplying virtually any good or service will lead to superior results in terms of improved quality, efficient production, and lower prices. When the good being supplied is a money, however, agreement about the benefits of competition is not universal. Even among economists, debates rage about whether economic systems in which currencies compete would lead to superior performance or to overissue and runaway inflation.[1]

I will argue that competition among suppliers of different monies is beneficial. To support that conclusion, I will review the case for competing currencies. I will discuss how increased competition among government-provided monies is already leading to lower inflation rates in developed economies. Finally, I will describe how privately supplied monies might enter the picture. I begin, however, with definitions and a brief discussion of the current role of central banks in supplying money to an economy.

What Is Money?

Articles about electronic money and "e-cash" abound. But as yet there seems to be no broad agreement about what electronic money is. Discussions of the subject include (and at times confuse) everything from whether or not credit card numbers can be securely

Catherine England is a faculty member in the Graduate Business Institute at George Mason University and President of England Economics.

[1]Although "currency" narrowly defined is the paper money we carry, we also use "currency" more broadly defined to refer to different types of money. Dollars, yen, francs, pounds, and Deutschemarks are thus different currencies. The focus of this paper might be more clearly described as competing monies.

transmitted over the Internet to the prospects for home banking to expanded opportunities for international transfers of financial assets. These questions (and many other similar issues) are all interesting, but this paper is concerned with who supplies the money used in an economy and whether the electronic revolution will change the supplier's identity.

But what is "money"? Money is what money does. We are particularly interested in money as a "medium of exchange."[2] In other words, "money" is anything I will accept in payment for goods or services because I can use the same money to buy what I want.

A single money (U.S. dollars, for example) may take different forms. Ask someone how much money she has, and she may count only the money in her wallet, she may think in terms of her checking account, or she may include balances in her savings account or investments in her stock mutual fund in arriving at a total.[3] Because of our emphasis on media of exchange, we will consider only readily spendable forms of money. In the United States (and other developed economies) money appears as both coins and currency (cash) and as checkable account balances, usually kept at banks and other depository institutions.

The central bank (the Federal Reserve System in the United States) is typically responsible for supplying the country's money. In economies where cash is the dominant form of money, the central bank has direct control over the domestic government-provided money supply, because the central bank determines how much money it will print.[4] In more developed economies, bank money (i.e., balances in checkable accounts) plays a more important role. As financial systems become more sophisticated and checkable account balances

[2]Money is typically viewed as having three characteristic functions. In addition to being a medium of exchange, money also represents a store of value and provides a unit of account. We will discuss the second and third functions below.

[3]In fact, government authorities use several definitions of money. The most narrow definition of money (M1) includes coins and currency in the hands of the public and checkable accounts. M2 includes M1 plus overnight repurchase agreements, overnight Eurodollar deposits, individuals' balances in money market mutual funds, balances in money market deposit accounts, savings deposits, and small (under $100,000) time deposits. M3 includes M2 and other less liquid balances.

[4]Cash is more important where the banking or payment processing systems of a country are less fully developed or (sometimes) where taxes or regulations are especially burdensome.

138

grow in importance, the central bank loses some of its control over the supply of the domestic money supply. Banks affect the money supply when they decide how much to lend.[5] As banks lend more, the money supply expands. When banks reduce their outstanding loans, the money supply contracts. The Federal Reserve can increase or decrease banks' capacity for making new loans, but the Fed cannot control banks' willingness to lend. As a result, the Federal Reserve does not exercise absolute control over the total number of dollars in the economy.[6]

Nor does any central bank exercise an absolute monopoly over the types of money in the domestic economy. Although government-supplied monies are most commonly used, if inflation becomes a serious problem, individuals in the economy may substitute other monies.[7] In some cases, buyers and sellers make exchanges using a currency from another country. The U.S. dollar and the German Deutschemark are both widely used outside their respective countries to buy and sell goods and services. But market participants need not turn just to other government-supplied currencies in the face of an unstable domestic money. After the collapse of the communist regime, prices in some Eastern European countries were quoted in quantities of rum, which could be used to buy a wide variety of other goods. As a practical matter, however, as long as the official government-sanctioned money represents a reasonable store of value (i.e., inflation is not too high), it enjoys an advantage over competing currencies in domestic transactions. After all, taxes are paid in government-sanctioned money.

---

[5]This is the case in countries with fractional reserve banking systems (which includes most countries). When a bank makes a loan, it increases the money available in the borrower's bank account without decreasing anyone else's bank account. Thus, the total amount of spendable money available in the economy increases.

[6]The Fed has three primary monetary policy tools: reserve requirements, the discount rate, and open market operations. Of these, open market operations are the most important. When the Fed buys Treasury securities on the open market, it provides more reserves to the banking system and encourages increased lending and money supply growth. Conversely, when the Fed sells its Treasury securities on the open market, it reduces the reserves available to the banking system, making it more difficult for banks to lend.

[7]Substitute monies have also arisen when there were insufficient supplies of government-sanctioned currency provided.

Why Competing Currencies?

Supporters of government money monopolies express two general concerns about competing money regimes. They worry about inflation and about transactions costs. In economic models, competition among suppliers causes the quantity produced of a good to increase and the price of the good to fall to its cost of production (including a normal profit). But an excessive increase in the supply of money will cause inflation. Opponents of competitive private currencies express concern that competition would mean an expanding total money supply (and consequent inflation) until the value of each money unit fell to its cost of production. As advances in technology reduce the cost of producing money, opponents of competition argue, the money supply would expand ever faster, causing increasing price instability.

Proponents of government-supplied money also argue that a single money, like a single language, facilitates trade and reduces transactions costs. (Europeans who favor a single Europewide currency make this argument.) In an economy where the government provides a single recognizable currency, merchants need not worry about determining the value of funds tendered in payment for goods. Similarly, buyers know their money will be accepted by merchants. As evidence of the money's "natural monopoly" status, advocates of government-provided monies often point to the fact that all major economies have central banks and government-supplied currencies.

The arguments in favor of competing currencies are the arguments in favor of competition generally. F.A. Hayek (1976, 1978), Roland Vaubel (1986), Lawrence H. White (1984, 1989), and George Selgin (1988), among others, have argued that competing suppliers of currencies would be required to provide market participants with monies exhibiting the characteristics that are most widely desired. Users of monies are generally assumed to prefer monies that are widely accepted and provide a stable (or at least predictable) store of value.

Government currencies have generally achieved reasonably wide acceptance, at least domestically.[8] But a stable value has proved more elusive. Marjorie Deane and Robert Pringle (1994: 352–53) reported that from 1971 to 1991, the German Deutschemark lost

---

[8]There are of course exceptions, but having the power to declare a currency "legal tender" helps promote acceptance.

more than 52 percent of its value, and Germany had the *best* record. By 1991, the U.S. dollar had lost more than 70 percent of its 1971 value, and over the same 20-year period, the British pound lost more than 84 percent of its 1971 value.

In fact, proponents of competition see reduced inflation as one of the primary benefits of currency competition. Vaubel (1986: 928) explained that the argument that competition would lead to overissue and inflation "confuses the price of acquiring money (the inverse of the price level) with the price (opportunity cost) of holding money. . . . Since money is an asset to be held, demand for it depends on the price of holding it." The cost of holding money rises as it loses purchasing power through inflation. Given a choice, market participants presumably would prefer to make exchanges and settle contracts (especially contracts with payments in the future) with a more reliable store of value.

Conventional wisdom holds, of course, that, when they existed, privately provided currencies were not "good" monies. "Wildcat banking" is the term most frequently associated with private banks' issuing competing bank notes in the United States. Banks were said to locate where only the wildcats could find them, thereby slowing the rate at which their bank notes could be returned and exchanged for gold or silver coins.

Merchants recognized that it might be difficult to obtain payment in good funds from unknown banks, of course, and they accepted notes from those banks only at a discount. Discounts depended on the reputation of the bank and the ease with which the notes could be exchanged for gold. Money brokers arose to buy bank notes from merchants and travelers and return the notes to their issuing banks for payment in gold. The brokers published lists of banks and the discounts (if any) attached to their notes.

Individuals and businesses accepting payment in notes from an unknown bank did need to invest in information about the market value of the notes, and market participants sometimes received less purchasing power or a poorer store of value than they had expected when they accepted particular notes in payment for some good or service.[9] But scholars taking a closer look at privately supplied currencies have not found the chaotic monetary conditions long

---

[9]Of course, the same has been true of government-issued monies.

assumed to have existed.[10] Arthur Rolnick and Warren Weber (1986: 887–88) observed, for example, that relevant information about the health and business practices of banks was more widely available during the 19th century than it is today. As a result, bank runs were not the random events they have often been pictured. They were targeted to institutions with serious solvency problems.[11] Lynne Doti and Larry Schweikart (1987) found in their study of banking in Western states that newly arrived bankers generally had to live in a community for several years and establish a reputation for honesty in some other line of business before they could attract deposits. Substantial bank buildings with expensive safes were not only a means of discouraging external thieves. They also provided a form of tangible, illiquid, immovable capital investment that a dishonest banker would of necessity forfeit if he left town.

Difficulties that did arise with privately issued currencies were often the result of government restrictions on private arrangements. Widespread government-imposed branching restrictions made it possible for less soundly managed banks to survive because stronger banks were unable to expand by opening new offices. Still, as long as banks were allowed to issue distinctive notes, overissue was limited both because distinctive notes could be readily returned to the issuing bank and because there was a real benefit to a bank's building "name brand capital" as a supplier of "quality" bank notes that traded at par.[12] Governments' subsequent requirements that banks issue uniform currencies increased banks' ability to overissue notes because the overissuing banks could not be as readily identified and their notes returned to them. Similarly, government efforts to force all bank notes and checks to trade at par reduced the market's discipline of less financially stable banks.[13]

[10]See, for example, Rockoff (1975), Rolnick and Weber (1986), and Dowd (1992).

[11]See also Kaufman (1988).

[12]Interestingly, banks that established a reputation for promptly paying gold for notes returned to them often found that their notes began to circulate longer (were returned less quickly) as they became more widely accepted as a reliable store of value.

[13]Gresham's (oft-quoted, but typically misunderstood) Law, "Bad money drives out good," applies only in markets with government enforced fixed exchange rates where the "bad" money is overvalued relative to the good. Requirements that all bank notes circulate at face value (which fixed the exchange rate) meant that notes issued by less sound banks (the "bad" money) was overvalued relative to money issued by sound banks (i.e., "good" money).

In short, private, competitive note issues did provide a stable source of money in many different economic settings.[14] Government-sponsored monies came to prevail, however, as governments sought to obtain for themselves the profits and advantages accruing to a monopoly supplier of money.

For a long time, governments were able to secure their money monopolies by fixing exchange rates, restricting international capital flows, limiting citizens' holdings of foreign currencies, and discouraging domestic market participants from writing contracts payable in an outside currency. Rapid advances in computer and communications technologies have reduced governments' ability to control international flows of funds, and increasingly government-sanctioned currencies are competing in international capital markets.

Competition Among Governments

In their book, *The Central Banks*, Deane and Pringle (1994) identified the removal of exchange rate controls as the point at which government-issued currencies began to compete with one another. As Deane and Pringle (ibid.: 325) observed, "[National currencies] were still issued by central banks with a monopoly of issuing high-powered money—bank reserves—denominated in the national currency, but there was less and less compulsion on anybody actually to use a given currency." Expanding world trade and rapidly developing international capital markets are also contributing to increasing capital mobility.

In a survey article on "The World Economy," the October 7, 1995 *Economist* described how changes during the past 20 years have altered international capital markets. As communications technology has advanced, the *Economist* argued, the world's financial markets have begun to evolve from a collection of individual domestic markets to a single massive global capital market. In this global capital market, investors shop any number of countries for desirable additions to their securities portfolios. The value of a security is clearly influenced by the stability of the currency in which the security is denominated.

---

[14]Dowd (1992), for example, examines private note issue in Australia, Canada, Colombia, Foochow (China), France, Ireland, Scotland, Switzerland, and the United States.

143

This increasing competition for financial capital is placing growing constraints on policymakers. Richard O'Brien (1995) observed that governments that attempt to tax too heavily (either explicitly or implicitly) see businesses shift their production to other countries. Governments that attempt to borrow too much or that allow their currencies to be devalued through inflation see investors flee with their funds looking for safer financial havens. The growing amount of financial capital that responds decisively to unsound government policy initiatives has forced government decisionmakers to consider the reactions of financial markets before introducing major new policy initiatives. The *Economist* survey quoted James Carville, an advisor to President Clinton: "I used to think that if there was reincarnation, I wanted to come back as the president or the pope. But now I want to be the bond market: you can intimidate everybody."

The transition to a single capital market is not complete, but it is far enough advanced that government decisionmakers are bemoaning their loss of control over their domestic economies. As Deane and Pringle (1994: 326) remarked, "Central banks are beginning to behave more like privately owned firms without actually being privatized."

Financial capital can only become more mobile as the information age advances. Practical barriers to individuals and businesses maintaining accounts with institutions in other countries will continue to fall. Why would I not store my wealth in a currency that retains (or increases) its value if moving funds to another location or another money requires only a few instructions delivered through my computer any time day or night? David Bollier (1996: 29) reported that First Direct, a bank based in Leeds, England, has attracted 500,000 on-line customers over the past five years. In the United States, Security First Network Bank of Pineville, Kentucky, has no physical branches. Its customers mail in deposits and access their accounts over the Internet. Other banks are exploring on-line banking services as is American Express, a nonbanking company. It is easy to imagine a worldwide bank offering accounts and loans in a variety of currencies. It is already beginning to happen. The physical offices of such a bank could exist almost anywhere—or nowhere if employees of the bank telecommute from locations in different countries around the world.

Enter Private Monies?

There are those who argue that bankers already supply private money. The vast majority of the money supplies of developed countries is found in the account balances of banks. But banks are regulated by the government, and they are subject to central bank reserve requirements. In thinking about private monies that compete with Federal Reserve-issued dollars, there are two paths to explore. The first path considers nonbank institutions, not subject to oversight by the central bank, creating additional spendable funds in much the same way banks do today. The funds created would still be "dollars" just as spendable funds generated by banks' lending activities are dollars. The second path to private money creation would involve a more direct challenge to the monetary authority, because a private supplier of this alternative would promote use of its money by pointing to its superiority as a more stable store of value, a more widely accepted medium of exchange, or an improved unit of account.

New Sources of Dollar Creation

Suppose a nonbank company that currently issues credit cards offers to parents of college students a prepaid debit card that can be "charged" at the beginning of the semester with funds to pay for everything from telephone calls to gasoline, groceries, rent, tuition, and books. If the card's sponsor (call the company National Express) takes the funds it receives from parents and invests those funds in loans to businesses, National Express has effectively created money. To the college students and their parents, the balances remaining on their debit cards are "money." But the businesses receiving the loans also have "money" they can spend. More spendable funds are available after National Express makes the loan than before the loan is made. National Express would no doubt look at its business loans as just a way to invest idle funds. It might not intend to challenge the monetary authority or serve as a source of "money creation." But create money, it has.

Some observers argue that any organization creating spendable balances in this manner should be subject to Federal Reserve oversight, especially Federal Reserve reserve requirements. The two most commonly cited reasons for subjecting these institutions to federal supervision are (1) to maintain the Fed's control over the money supply, and (2) to enable the Fed to act decisively if a nonbank, money creating institution should fail.

If nonbank institutions do begin to create money, the Fed's direct control of the money supply would appear to be diminished. But as noted, the Fed's control over the money supply today is not complete. Money creation depends on households' willingness to leave their funds in banks and banks' willingness to lend. With or without nonbank institutions creating money, the Fed will be forced to monitor economic conditions and overall credit creation and focus its efforts on affecting total liquidity through open market operations. There is not a strong argument for the Fed's regulating nonbank institutions as a means of consolidating its control of the U.S. money supply.

The Fed's feeling a need to intervene if a nonbank institution should fail would indicate either explicit or implicit access by the failed institution's creditors to the deposit insurance safety net. But the creditors of National Express (the college students' parents who had deposited funds against which the debit card would draw) should not receive federal guarantees. First, taxpayers' insurance obligations should not be extended further. Second, forcing new nonbank institutions to develop without deposit insurance (or other similar guarantees) would ensure that these institutions represented a real alternative to commercial banks.

I have argued that the introduction of federal deposit insurance in 1934 stunted the development of more stable forms of banking by shifting to the government the risk of bank runs and failures. The advantages of a more stable banking system to both depositors and bank owners and managers are substantial in the absence of government guarantees. Without deposit insurance, new contractual arrangements or different security mechanisms would surely have developed as market participants searched for stability. The dramatic failures of the 1980s as well as central bankers' continuing concern about the fragility of the financial system would seem to indicate government guarantees have not solved the stability problem.

With the advent of new sources of money creation, we have an opportunity to see where market developments will take us. Nonbank money-creating institutions could well be subject to runs, just as banks are.[15] If nonbank institutions want to create money, they should be left on their own to establish contractual terms and security arrangements necessary to reassure customers.[16] Institutions that want federal guarantees could apply for bank charters. But if the Fed simply extends either explicit or implicit guarantees to the creditors of nonbank institutions, bank-like regulation would almost certainly follow. Regulating nonbank financial institutions like banks would reduce the innovation and experimentation taking place in U.S. financial markets, and we might miss an opportunity to discover a superior banking arrangement.

New Types of Money

New types of money are unlikely to arise in the absence of substantial dissatisfaction with existing government-sponsored monies. So the creator of a new money might arise in the face of substantial inflation. Of course the money entrepreneur would need to find a way to provide a credible promise that his privately issued money would maintain its value where the government money had not. Some commentators have envisioned the development of separate "cyberspace" monies as a means of avoiding taxes. If a bank or other financial institution has no physical offices, how could government regulators or tax collectors enforce a demand to review the institution's books? The task becomes more complex if account balances are reported and payments made and received in some new cyberspace credit. Then again, new types of money might represent nothing more than a convenience. Our worldwide bank offering accounts in different currencies could conceivably create a completely new unit of account in which to keep its records. Deposits and withdrawals in government currencies would be translated into Planet Bank monetary unit equivalents. From there it is a short step to contracts written and fulfilled in Planet Bank units rather than in yen, francs,

---

[15]This is because money-creating financial institutions typically do not have enough readily liquidated assets to meet all their outstanding liabilities should all their creditors demand immediate payment.

[16]England (1988) describes many of the arrangements used by uninsured bankers historically to reassure customers.

or dollars.[17] While advances in communications technology may dramatically change the terms under which market transactions take place, I believe historical episodes of private monies can provide some insights into what a 21st century private money would look like.

Any money depends first on trust. Private (and public) issuers of money in the future will be required to establish their reliability in delivering payment services through mechanisms that meet the needs of users. Marvin Sirbu, a professor with the Information Network Institute at Carnegie Mellon University, has observed: "All money depends upon trust in my ability to issue an instruction to move money from one place to another" (Bollier 1996: 26). Moving money essentially involves an instruction to the "keepers of the books." Buyers and sellers must believe that "money" exists in the repository that receives the payment instruction, that the instruction to make a payment will be faithfully executed, and that the identity of the payor and the payee can be authenticated.

But how do we know that the "keepers of the books," whether they are regulated commercial banks or institutions that exist in cyberspace, have money with which to make payments? Historically, money was first something that had value in itself (tobacco, animal hides). Then currencies convertible to something of value (usually gold) were developed. Today's fiat currencies are backed only by governments' promises to control their supply, but at least we can hold fiat currencies in our hands. What happens as electronic forms of money become increasingly important? Regulated commercial banks keep their money balances as cash in the vault or (primarily) as accounts with the Federal Reserve System. Thus, the central bank vouches for their having "money balances."

Users of privately created cyberspace monetary units would also no doubt insist on some independent verification that the "money" did in fact exist. Trusted, third-party guarantors might thus develop to verify the presence of reserves or assets necessary to make payments. Cyberspace credits would almost certainly be payable (at the

---

[17]Speculation about a Planet Bank monetary unit may remind readers of efforts by countries in the European Union to create a European-wide currency. The difference is that a private international monetary unit would have to gain acceptance among money users by displaying valued characteristics. It would not be imposed by government authorities.

depositor's discretion) in something other than just more cyberspace credits. For our Planet Bank described above, the newly created monetary unit might be payable in the depositor's choice of any of a number of government-issued currencies. Another contract might develop whereby a cyberspace customer could receive payment in any of a list of financial assets—U.S. Treasury securities, Aaa corporate bonds, or gold futures, for example. The formulas for converting cyberspace monetary units to either government currencies or to other financial assets would be established up front.[18]

Historically, successful issuers of money often had to do more than just make a promise to convert their bank notes into gold. They often needed a physical presence in the town, someplace customers could go to receive payment. Furthermore, successful "new" bankers often had already established reputations in a nonbank line of business so that customers felt they knew with whom they were dealing. Will market participants require similar reassuring structures before accepting new monies in the coming century? It is widely expected that home banking using personal computers will allow banks to close large numbers of physical branches as we move into the 21st century. Will customers continue to demand to be able to meet with bank representatives face to face when there is a problem or a question? And if trust is a prerequisite to introducing new monetary services, what companies will become the new money entrepreneurs? Will totally new entrants find ways to reassure market participants about their trustworthiness? Or will we only use new monies and payment systems offered by corporations and institutions with recognized, established reputations?

There are also many questions about the terms in which new monies might be denominated. To truly compete with government-issued money, users would have to be able to distinguish privately issued currencies from dollars, pounds, and lira. That would make it more difficult to denominate new monies in terms of the government-sanctioned monies, but it would not necessarily be impossible.

---

[18]Treasury bond futures contracts are based on an artificial bond with a standardized (and constant) coupon rate and maturity. When Treasury bond futures contracts come due, those owners of futures contracts who do not cash settle can choose from one of several actual bonds to meet the delivery requirements of the contract. Conversion formulas for different types of bonds are established and agreed to by all market participants up front.

During the 19th century, privately issued bank notes in the United States were all denominated in dollars, for example. Notes issued by less sound banks simply circulated at a discount. Perhaps dollar-denominated private money issued by (say) American Express would circulate at a premium if it came to represent a superior store of value to U.S. government dollars.

Finally, F. X. Browne and David Cronin (1995), among others, foresee mutual funds becoming the basis for privately issued monies. Mutual fund-based money would eliminate any reason for runs to develop, and proponents argue it thus provides a superior basis for supplying transactions balances.[19] This could be one of the new, superior forms of bank contracts that develop, but my guess is that many individuals and businesses will want their transactions account to maintain a fixed (or growing, but not fluctuating) value.

Conclusion

Hayek once observed, "The history of government management of money has, except for a few short happy periods, been one of incessant fraud and deception."[20] Sounding a similar theme in the conclusion to their book on central banks, Deane and Pringle (1994: 346) wrote, "Trust in money depends above all on controlling the power of the state." Throughout history, governments have used their control over the money supply to periodically exact inflation taxes. But governments' ability to maintain a monopoly over their money supplies appears to be fading fast.

Businesses, financial institutions, and individual investors are becoming ever more comfortable moving among currencies as they look for investments and seek out loans. A growing number of businesses and households have bank accounts denominated in foreign currencies as they search for both convenience and improved returns on their investments. Increasingly, central banks are forced to act as competitors or see their currencies, their financial markets, and their economies bypassed by the world's market participants. As a result, residents of developed countries are already enjoying

---

[19]Because mutual fund shares are constantly marked to market, there is no advantage to being first in line to receive your funds.

[20]Quoted in Wriston (1995).

improved price stability. There is even evidence that the U.S. Treasury Department is feeling the competitive heat as it is finally moving
to offer inflation indexed bonds.

The new question is whether competition will also arise from
the private sector. (More precisely, the question is whether private
sources of money will pose a serious competitive challenge to government-sanctioned monies.) Advancing technology will make it
increasingly difficult for government agents to regulate or tax private
monies out of existence as they have in the past. Even if courts or
government regulators declare certain financial assets as "out of
bounds," enforcing those decisions may prove impossible if suppliers of the new currencies cross national boundaries or have no
physical location against which government actions can take place.
What is "money" will be determined by what buyers and sellers
accept and use as money rather than by government definitions.

For the time being at least, government-sanctioned money and
traditional banking arrangements will enjoy the benefit of the doubt
because of their familiarity, if for no other reason. But market participants may prove impatient if government arrangements prove themselves untrustworthy. Real alternatives will be readily at hand.

In *The Future of Electronic Commerce*, Bollier (1996: 24) wrote,
"Money is as much a social convention as an object or technology.
Its use value in a given form depends critically upon widespread
acceptance of that form." He then quoted Dee Hock, founder and
CEO emeritus of Visa International: "At bottom, [electronic value
exchange] is an institutional problem, not a technical one. It is about
developing a set of relationships among the players and creating
guarantees of absolute trust." In a similar vein, Deane and Pringle
(1994: 346) quoted Herbert Frankel of Oxford University: "The
debate about the future of money is not about inflation or deflation,
fixed or flexible exchange rates, gold or paper standards; it is about
the kind of society in which money is to operate." If the debates
over the future of money are any indication, the future may hold
increasing promise of freedom and choice for Wall Street financiers,
Florida retirees, and everyone between.

References

Bollier, D., rapporteur (1996) *The Future of Electronic Commerce*. Washington,
D.C.: The Aspen Institute.

Browne, F.X., and Cronin, D. (1995) "Payments Technologies, Financial Innovation and Laissez-Faire Banking." *Cato Journal* 15 (Spring/Summer): 101–16.

Deane, M., and Pringle, R. (1994) *The Central Banks.* New York: Viking Penguin.

Doti, L.P., and Schweikart, L. (1987) "Western Frontier Banking: Symbols of Safety." Paper presented at the Western Economics Association meetings, Vancouver, B. C., July.

Dowd, K., ed. (1992) *The Experience of Free Banking.* London: Routledge.

England, C. (1988) "Agency Costs and Unregulated Banks: Could Depositors Protect Themselves?" In C. England and T. Huertas (eds.) *The Financial Services Revolution: Policy Directions for the Future*, 317–43. Boston: Kluwer.

Hayek, F.A. (1976) *Choice in Currency: A Way to Stop Inflation.* London: Institute of Economic Affairs.

Hayek, F.A. (1978) *Denationalisation of Money — The Argument Refined: An Analysis of the Theory and Practice of Concurrent Currencies.* 2d ed. London: Institute of Economic Affairs.

Kaufman, G.G. (1988) "The Truth about Bank Runs." In C. England and T. Huertas (eds.) *The Financial Services Revolution: Policy Directions for the Future*, 9–40. Boston: Kluwer.

O'Brien, R. (1995) "Who Rules the World's Financial Markets?" *Harvard Business Review* (March/April).

Rockoff, H. (1975) *The Free Banking Era: A Re-examination.* New York: Arno Press.

Rolnick, A.J., and Weber, W.E. (1986) "Inherent Instability in Banking: The Free Banking Experience." *Cato Journal* 5 (Winter): 877–90.

Selgin, G.A. (1988) *The Theory of Free Banking: Money Supply under Competitive Note Issue.* Totowa, N.J.: Rowman and Littlefield.

Vaubel, R. (1986) "Currency Competition versus Governmental Money Monopolies." *Cato Journal* 5 (Winter): 927–42.

White, L.H. (1984) *Free Banking in Britain: Theory, Experience and Debate, 1800–1845.* New York: Cambridge University Press.

White, L.H. (1989) *Competition and Currency: Essays on Free Banking and Money.* New York: New York University Press.

Woodall, P. (1995) "The World Economy: Who's in the Driving Seat?" *The Economist* (Survey), 7 October.

Wriston, W. (1995) "Money: Back to Future?" *Wall Street Journal*, 24 November: A8.

19

PAYMENT TECHNOLOGIES, FINANCIAL INNOVATION, AND LAISSEZ-FAIRE BANKING: A FURTHER DISCUSSION OF THE ISSUES

F. X. Browne and David Cronin

Laissez-faire banking literature is based on the premises that the market is better at allocating resources than government and that there is nothing fundamentally different about the provision of money and banking services relative to the provision of other goods and services that should invite "special" government intervention in the banking industry. That literature has tended to focus on private banks issuing traditional notes and coin. We have sought to complement that body of research by giving greater attention to the potential implications of electronic payment instruments that are currently being developed by private-sector firms. Those implications are discussed in our recent article in the *Cato Journal* (Browne and Cronin 1995). The underlying theme of that paper is that advances in electronic payments, in conjunction with innovations in financial products, would appear capable of delivering a laissez-faire banking system that would be both inherently stable and beneficial to macroeconomic performance.

In this paper, we summarize the arguments made in our *Cato Journal* paper and discuss further some of the key issues in this area. In particular, we look more closely at how technology might affect

Frank Browne is an advisor in the Economic Analysis, Research and Publications Department at the Central Bank of Ireland. He is also Deputy Head of Stage III Division of the MES Department at the European Monetary Institute in Frankfurt, Germany. David Cronin is an economist at the Central Bank of Ireland and is currently on leave from the Bank to Sheffield Hallam University. The views expressed in this paper are not necessarily held by the Central Bank of Ireland nor by the European Monetary Institute and are the sole responsibility of the authors.

the future shape of banking and what role government regulation might play in banking in the future. We conclude that laissez-faire banking could emerge endogenously over time in response to technological improvements in information and financial products; that regulation of this "new" banking industry could prove extremely costly for government to undertake; and that, irrespective of whether government is inclined or not to do so, any attempts to regulate would be unjustified because of the system's likely inherent stability and efficiency.

Electronic Payments and the Demise of Outside Currency

Our view that laissez-faire banking could emerge endogenously in the future is grounded in the pecuniary and nonpecuniary advantages that new electronic payments technologies are likely to have over government-issued currency. Those advantages will extend to all parties who use currency for transactions purposes. For banks, electronic payments promise to be very cost efficient in comparison to prevailing paper-based payments systems. A switch from paper to electronic media is likely to cut deep inroads into bank costs, particularly labor costs, of routine processing of currency and paper-based payment instruments. Retailers would benefit from a switch to electronic payments by not having to carry or handle large physical sums of currency, which would also reduce their costs and susceptibility to theft. Electronic payments are likely to prove attractive to consumers as well. In particular, there is the potential pecuniary advantage of earning interest on unspent electronic purchasing power. In the case of smart cards with embedded value, the logistics of the issuer paying interest on the unspent balances are simple. (As Lawrence H. White [1995] has pointed out, this could be achieved by programming the card's microchip to augment the unspent card balance automatically over time.) Where electronic payments are effected on-line to an interest-bearing bank account, the payment of interest would be obviously very straightforward.

For all the aforementioned parties, the technology would also have the benefit of allowing instant verification of a payer's creditworthiness, unlike pay-later payment media such as credit cards. Thus, the hitherto distinct advantage of government currency over privately issued paper-based payment instruments in allowing immediate verification of the creditworthiness of the payer could be mitigated with the arrival of new privately issued electronic payment instruments.

Given these advantages, it is not unreasonable to argue that electronic payments could substitute strongly for currency and other paper-based instruments. It is difficult to see how those paper media could undergo any improvements that would allow them to compete with electronic media. Networking effects are also likely to play an important part in the spread of new electronic payments technologies. The usefulness of any particular payments product to an individual is an increasing function of the number of individuals who already use and accept it in executing transactions. If that number is small the benefit to the marginal individual of choosing the new instrument is also going to be small given the low number of other agents utilizing the instrument.[1] If the number of users is large, or growing rapidly, then the incentive to start utilizing and accepting the instrument in payments will correspondingly increase. This type of networking effect could give rise to important nonlinearities in the rate at which new payments products spread throughout the economy. There could be large inertial effects initially preventing the demand for a new payments product taking off, but once it does take off it could experience exponential growth. If demand does not reach a critical mass, the instrument may never succeed. But once this critical mass has been reached the use of the payments product will be diffused very rapidly and should quickly displace other existing, but inferior, products. Predictions of the rate at which new electronic payments products will grow and replace currency that do not take account of such networking effects may be quite misleading.[2]

Some observers might argue that, irrespective of the technological and economic superiority of electronic payment media, consumers will continue to utilize paper-based instruments with which they are familiar and which they trust. Certainly, such inertia might be

---

[1]Caskey and Sellon (1994) identify difficulties of this nature (along with the pricing of payment methods) as an impediment to debit card growth.

[2]Stix (1993) makes the point that the diffusion of a technology often accelerates as costs drop. In particular, he shows how products such as the telephone, the personal computer, and the videocassette recorder penetrated the U.S. consumer market as their costs fell exponentially. A similar situation might be expected to develop with regard to the new payment technologies.

expected in the short- to medium-term. It might be particularly strong among older generations. Younger generations, however, are likely to trust and use new technology so that this source of inertia might disappear within a few decades. Yet, the initial strength of the inertia might be in itself exaggerated because, as Tom Kokkola and Raul Pauli (1994: 7) argue,

> In principle, the introduction of electronic cash constitutes a far less dramatic change than the introduction of paper money [as a replacement for metallic money] since it really only involves a change in the form of the "instrument" representing purchasing power. What paper money and electronic money share in common then is that the monetary status of both is based on the holder's confidence that the issuer will meet his obligations under all circumstances.

Growing familiarity over time with new payments products should tend to reduce gradually people's natural reluctance to trust payments products that they may not fully understand. The mere demonstration of their durability and viability by some agents should be enough to encourage others to use and accept the new payments products. This is not a networking effect as such but would nevertheless tend to operate in the same highly nonlinear way in its impact on the usage of electronic payments.

For these reasons, we believe that government-issued currency may experience a substantial decline or even disappear as a transactions medium in the long run with seigniorage passing to the private sector in the form of a cheaper and more efficient payments system, unless these competitive advantages were somehow countered by central banks. That would appear unlikely since, as already noted, it is difficult to envisage currency undergoing any technological improvement that would allow it to counter the attractions of electronic money. Should central banks seek to engage in the supply of electronic money they are likely to be frustrated in their attempts to do so, because electronic payments technology is already well-disbursed among private institutions and central banks have little expertise in retail banking. In our view, therefore, central banks are unlikely to become direct issuers of electronic money.

Regulation of Electronic Payments

An outright prohibition by central banks on electronic money issue by private banks to sustain demand for its own (paper) currency is not likely to arise. For one thing, such a prohibition might prove politically sensitive, particularly if electronic money has garnered a significant popularity among the public. Second, many central banks appear willing to accept that consumers should be free to choose their own preferred payment medium.[3]

Furthermore, any attempt to regulate the electronic money industry might prove to be futile for central banks. Electronic purse schemes, now being operated on either a pilot or fully operational basis in many countries, might be easily regulated because they are mainly being operated by resident banks with a large physical presence in a country. Payments services that are being provided via the Internet are, however, likely to prove far more difficult to regulate. The Internet is an information network that has no physical presence and recognizes no national barriers. Even if a government succeeded in regulating the activities of Internet payment service providers in its jurisdiction, it is likely that consumers could turn to other service providers based abroad in order to avail of, for example, superior interest-earning opportunities being offered by those foreign operators. Any attempt by regulatory authorities to exercise influence on the domestic nonbank public could also prove futile since cryptographic procedures and the multiplicity of transmission paths available on the Internet would make the cost of any effective attempts to regulate those agents' behavior excessively costly.[4]

An attempt by regulatory authorities to prevent its supervisees from providing electronic payment facilities to their customers could threaten to reduce the supervisees' customer base as less-regulated institutions would be free to provide such payment facilities. Indeed, in order to preserve the systemic health of their constituencies (and the public perception of the success of their own regulatory activity), regulatory authorities would most likely be forced to rescind their

---

[3]The Working Group on EU Payment Systems (1994: 7), for instance, states that "EU central banks are of the opinion that the market should decide which payment instruments best serve customer needs."

[4]The nature of the Internet could make it difficult for central banks to quantify the amount of effective transactions balances within the economy. With imperfect information on the amount of money in circulation in the country, or on the velocity of such money, the ability of the central bank to pursue a monetary policy strategy of intermediate monetary targeting would be compromised.

own regulation that restricted their "clients" from competing effectively with other firms in this area.[5]

Accounting System of Exchange and the Unit of Account

There is, we would argue, considerable potential for on-line electronic payments technology to impact on how exchange in the economy takes place. Specifically, it seems capable of making an accounting system of exchange (ASE) a viable challenger and alternative to the current ubiquitous monetary exchange system.[6] In the future it could be possible to settle transactions by means of signals to an electronic accounting network resulting in appropriate credits and debits to agents' bank accounts. Ownership of security claims could be transferred to settle transactions. Such an exchange system would correspond to an ASE. In monetary exchange systems, the basic medium of exchange (be that commodity money or fiat money) invariably has served as the unit of account. In a situation where there is no tangible medium of exchange, the choice of the unit of account becomes less obvious. New monetary economics theorists, who have considered how an exchange system based on (intrinsic) book-entry transfers of wealth to settle transactions might function, have argued that a unit of account based on some quantity of a commodity or bundle of commodities would be required in an ASE.

In considering the possible demise of currency as a transaction medium in the context of a movement toward a cashless economy, based on the technologies described above, we believe that currency's unit of account function need not necessarily be undermined.

---

[5]This argument is somewhat similar to the viewpoint of Edward Kane (1983) on the nature of regulatory activity.

[6]Prepaid cards, because purchasing power is embedded in the card and can only be transferred by possession and physical utilization of that instrument, are bearer instruments. Those instruments, by definition, do not embrace book entry in the settlement of transactions and are, therefore, monetary rather than ASE payment instruments. Payments made on the Internet involve settlement of transactions by book entry. Similarly, debit cards are used to initiate account-to-account transfers and, thus, are compatible with an ASE.

On a related point, David Everett (1996) has pointed out that electronic purses such as Mondex are as fungible as cash insofar as payment flows can take place in a bi-directional flow between (initial) payer and payee. In contrast, book-entry type exchange must involve immediate exchange of assets between the payer's bank and the payee's bank so that all payment flows operate unidirectionally.

So long as a demand for currency prevails, it will continue to have a positive and determinate value relative to other goods and consequently will continue to be capable of serving as a viable unit of account. Even if the demand for currency as a medium of exchange were to disappear, it is likely that an alternative demand for that currency as a store of value would remain, such as a demand among numismatists to hold particular fiat note and coin issues and among agents in other, less developed countries in search of "hard" currency to hold as a store of value.

The Future of Banking

We have argued that technological developments may, in the long run, lead to payments services being fully provided by an unregulated private sector utilizing electronic technology. Providing payment facilities to its customers has been one of the two key functions that banks have undertaken within the economy; the other is intermediating funds between savers and investors. Both functions are no longer the sole preserve of banks, however. Mutual funds and brokerage firms now compete with banks in financial intermediation. The number of nonbanks seeking to enter the market for providing payment facilities by exploiting the opportunities that the new information technologies present is also growing.

Does this threaten banking and banks? On the one hand, banks seem certain to face greater competition with the advent of sophisticated information and financial products. On the other hand, it is difficult to see the business of banking being undermined, if one takes banking's central quality to be its ability to help solve information asymmetries in the intermediation process. We would expect that banks will continue to earn fee income in reducing the cost and risk of intermediation, irrespective of who originates the funds to make a loan or what liability remains with the bank. Banks' credit assessing skills might be expected, for example, to be in demand from nonbank electronic payment service providers choosing to enter the area of intermediation of funds. Given that those "digital banks" would have little or no prior knowledge of banking and that banking may be "special" insofar as banks have unique access to information about their clients' activities, the model of share banking might prove the only feasible option for those new banks to follow in engaging in intermediation. This is because their inexperience of the

159

banking business would not prove costly to them if those agents saving with them, rather than themselves, bore the default risk associated with loans. This could be achieved through securitization, which involves financial intermediaries extending loans to borrowers as per traditional (par-value) intermediation but, unlike that form of intermediation, pooling those loans and selling claims on this pool to savers. In addition, they would not be required to engage in risk assessment of ultimate issuers (in which they have no experience), because that function is already being done by underwriters (for example, merchant banks) in the case of new issues and by the market in the case of outstanding issues.

Competition in this new banking environment might be expected to be strong. If data and payment transmission could be made at negligible marginal cost, geography would be irrelevant in the provision of banking services so that a strong horizontal dimension to competition in banking would exist. Also, almost by definition, the Internet removes the need for intermediaries in the transmission of information. It is difficult to believe how this should not also apply to banking on the Internet, particularly if it is securitized claims that are exchanged therein. With securitized claims, there would seem to be no need for clearinghouses (which formed an integral element in the institutional development of monetary payment systems) in an ASE. That is because there would be no need to hold quantities of a noninterest-bearing asset (final money) as the ultimate settlement medium, and because all transactions would be settled in real time on a bilateral, rather than a multilateral, basis. The absence of an institution such as a clearinghouse, with a unique function in the payment system, would remove any focal point for government regulation. Indeed, recognition of that fact should remove any inclination on private institutions' part to form a central organization for clearing payments. The impact of the new technologies, therefore, may be to weaken, and perhaps, fully remove government regulation of financial intermediation and payments; the cost of direct monitoring of intermediary activity and implementation of supervisory rules could end up being excessively large and could put regulatees at a distinct disadvantage to their competitors.

We would argue that a banking system of the type described above, based on electronic payments and share banking, would be inherently stable. Laissez-faire in electronic payments could compare favorably with free-banking note and coin issue. The stability of bank liability issue could be strengthened by the mechanism of adverse clearing operating even more promptly in a payment system based on electronic funds transfer than on circulating physical currency.[7] Share banking can support stability in laissez-faire banking. In particular, as has been pointed out by David Glasner (1989) and George Selgin and Lawrence H. White (1994), runs are unlikely to be made on share banks.[8]

Selgin and White (1994: 1729), while acknowledging that runs cannot occur on share banks, argue that par-value banking would survive under laissez-faire because "it beneficially constrains banks to act in the interest of claimholders, precisely because claimholders have the option of forcing liquidation." We would argue that a similar constraint would operate on share banks. Savers in share banks do not have fixed nominal claims on those banks. This should lead them to monitor more closely the investment performance of those banks. Should a bank be making inferior investment choices, savers would most likely become more fully and more quickly informed of those poor choices in a share-banking environment than they would in a par-value system and would seek to divert existing (and new) savings to other banks; this could be achieved rapidly since all claims in share banks are liquid and are not subject to either term or period-of-notice constraints. Par-value deposits are, with the exception of sight deposits, subject to such constraints. This impedes the ability of depositors to force liquidation on those banks.[9]

The new electronic payments media, particularly on-line technology, could help to promote share banking. Using paper-based media

[7]The use of securitized claims for payments might also ease credit risks that payees might have with regard to both payers and their banks. Those claims would be marked-to-market on an ongoing basis and would be transferable instantaneously at the time of contract. Thus, electronic technology would ensure that there would be no delay in a payment obligation being made good with underlying real wealth. The creditworthiness of any counterparty to a transaction can be verified, the required funds transferred and the transaction settled with finality virtually instantaneously.

[8]The arguments supporting this view are more fully outlined in our *Cato Journal* article.

[9]Stephen Ross (1989) characterizes par-value intermediaries, such as savings and loan organizations, as opaque. Those are institutions for which "monitoring, bonding and control costs, i.e., agency problems, are most severe . . . .[A] depositor in an S&L has almost no knowledge of the particular loans the institution is making" (ibid.:

to settle transactions with shares in a bank is excessively costly (hence the existing demand for par-value notes and coin and sight deposits as settlement media). Electronic transfer of marked-to-market shares could prove, however, to be a cost-competitive alternative to payment by par-value notes and coin and sight deposits. This in itself could help promote share banking. Also, what is likely to be attractive to retail transactors about share banking is that all account holdings would be liquid and divisible. This contrasts with par-value banking deposits which tend (with the exception of sight deposits) to come with maturity bands or periods of notice. Since they are not negotiable, they cannot be mobilized for payments short of maturity except at a penalty. Transferring them to an alternative ownership may be impossible if deposits cannot be converted to notes and coin or a sight deposit or can only be converted to liquidity at a cost that is too large relative to the value of the transactions in question. This is not a problem with share banking since account holdings are all liquid and divisible. If banks wish to maximize their services to clients who have installed the required network infrastructure to support, say, a debit card system, banks would have a strong incentive to supply tradable marked-to-market financial instruments rather than medium-to-long maturity deposits.

Macroeconomic Behavior in an ASE

Legal restrictions imposed by government could be either circumvented or rescinded in the new banking environment. The end of the endogenous developments now being observed in their infancy could give substance to the central paradigm of the new monetary economics literature: "If legal restrictions explain the special role of money and banking [in economic activity], a world without such restrictions should be one in which money and banking are devoid of such special significance" (Harper and Coleman 1992: 29). Contributors to that literature (in particular, Fama [1980]) have argued that by maintaining bank liabilities at par, regulators give special significance to bank liability issue, insofar as the incentive for its

---

542). In contrast, he holds that participants in an open-ended mutual fund "at any moment of time. . . . can be fully informed about the assets of the fund. There is no substantial equity investment in the fund by those who manage it, and their principal compensation is a percentage of the assets under management . . . . there is less room for a divergence in interests between management and the participants."

continued issue is unlimited and that issue gives rise to ongoing inflation unless a quantity restriction is imposed by further regulation. If the initial restriction had not been imposed, then bank liability issue would have an impact on its own price. With a falling marginal profit from liability issue, any incentive for overissue would be eliminated. In this way there would be nothing "special" about bank liability issue; its equilibrium quantity would be determined by the orthodox demand and supply forces that operate in most goods markets.

In an ASE, signaling between economic agents could improve due to all wealth being liquid and perfectly divisible. Since all wealth, when combined with a secure electronic messaging transmission process, would be capable of acting as transactions media, there would be no need to hoard transaction balances in order to build up liquid savings to finance future expenditure plans, as is the case in monetary economies where only money (which represents a small proportion of total wealth) constitutes readily expendable balances. Thus, with no need to hoard in an ASE, current expenditure patterns would not need to be disrupted to build up a stock of transactions balances. Such hoarding activity has been identified as a means by which business cycles can arise since firms may mistakenly view the decline in consumer expenditures as permanent (rather than as an intertemporal readjustment of expenditures) so that they will tend to produce less output than will actually be demanded in the future. Such a coordination failure between producers and consumers would not arise in an ASE because its source, the need to build up liquid balances, would be mitigated.

Furthermore, as Cronin (1994: 55) notes, resource allocation would also be improved insofar as when agents observe price changes occurring they would be aware that those are specifically relative price changes (since changes in the aggregate price level do not arise in an ASE) and, consequently, agents would channel resources to more efficient uses in response to these signals.

Conclusion

In this paper, we have argued that new electronic payments media, being developed by private firms, could replace government-issued notes and coins and that laissez-faire banking could emerge endogenously from that technology. We believe that a banking industry

163

based on the model of share banking and electronic payments would be both efficient and stable and would prove conducive to improved economic performance. While technological developments might be expected to expose existing banks to strong competition in payments and intermediation, those banks are likely to continue to have both perceived and actual superior risk-assessing skills to new entrants in the intermediation business. This comparative advantage should ensure that they will continue to earn income by way of fee for their credit-rating skills, irrespective of whether all their other business activities prosper or fail in the new technological environment.

References

Browne, F.X., and Cronin, D. (1995) "Payment Technologies, Financial Innovation, and Laissez-Faire Banking." *Cato Journal* 15 (1): 101–16.

Caskey, J.P, and Sellon, G.H. Jr. (1994) "Is the Debit Card Revolution Finally Here?" Federal Reserve Bank of Kansas City *Economic Review* (fourth quarter): 79–95.

Cronin, D. (1994) "Patterns in Money Demand: Indicators and Predictions." Central Bank of Ireland *Technical Paper 8/RT/94*. Dublin, Ireland.

Everett, D. (1996) "A Security Comparison of Modern Electronic Payment Instruments." Paper presented at a conference on "The Cashless Economy" 28 March, Dublin, Ireland.

Fama, E. (1980) "Banking in the Theory of Finance." *Journal of Monetary Economics* 6: 39–57.

Glasner, D. (1989) *Free Banking and Monetary Reform.* Cambridge: Cambridge University Press.

Harper, I., and Coleman, A. (1992) "New Monetary Economics." In P. Newman, M. Milgate, and J. Eatwell (eds.) *New Palgrave Dictionary of Money and Finance*, Vol. 3: 28–31. New York: Stockton Press.

Kane, E.J. (1983) "Policy Implications of Structural Changes in Financial Markets." *American Economic Review* 73: 96–100.

Kokkola, T., and Pauli, R. (1994) "Electronic Cash." Bank of Finland *Bulletin* 12: 2–7. Helsinki, Finland.

Ross, S. (1989) "Institutional Markets, Financial Marketing, and Financial Innovation." *Journal of Finance* 44: 541–56.

Selgin, G., and White, L.H. (1994) "How Would the Invisible Hand Handle Money?" *Journal of Economic Literature* 32: 1718–49.

Stix, G. (1993) "Domesticating Cyberspace." *Scientific American* (August): 85–92.

White, L.H. (1995) "Thoughts on the Economics of Digital Currency." *Extropy* 15 (7)(2): 16–18.

Working Group on EU Payment Systems (1994) *Report to the Council of the European Monetary Institute on Prepaid Cards*. European Monetary Institute, Frankfurt-am-Main, Germany.

Index

ABOUT THE EDITOR

James A. Dorn is Vice President for Academic Affairs at the Cato Institute, Editor of the *Cato Journal*, and Professor of Economics at Towson State University. He directs Cato's annual Monetary Conference and is coeditor of *The Search for Stable Money; Dollars, Deficits, and Trade; Monetary Reform in Post-Communist Countries;* and *Money and Markets in the Americas*. Dorn has taught at the Central European University in Prague and has lectured at Fudan University in Shanghai. His articles have appeared in the *Financial Times*, the *Washington Times*, the *Boston Herald*, the *Journal of Commerce*, and the *Dallas Morning News*. He holds a M.A. and Ph.D. in economics from the University of Virginia. From 1984–90, he served on the White House Commission on Presidential Scholars.

Cato Institute

Founded in 1977, the Cato Institute is a public policy research foundation dedicated to broadening the parameters of policy debate to allow consideration of more options that are consistent with the traditional American principles of limited government, individual liberty, and peace. To that end, the Institute strives to achieve greater involvement of the intelligent, concerned lay public in questions of policy and the proper role of government.

The Institute is named for *Cato's Letters*, libertarian pamphlets that were widely read in the American Colonies in the early 18th century and played a major role in laying the philosophical foundation for the American Revolution.

Despite the achievement of the nation's Founders, today virtually no aspect of life is free from government encroachment. A pervasive intolerance for individual rights is shown by government's arbitrary intrusions into private economic transactions and its disregard for civil liberties.

To counter that trend, the Cato Institute undertakes an extensive publications program that addresses the complete spectrum of policy issues. Books, monographs, and shorter studies are commissioned to examine the federal budget, Social Security, regulation, military spending, international trade, and myriad other issues. Major policy conferences are held throughout the year, from which papers are published thrice yearly in the *Cato Journal*. The Institute also publishes the quarterly magazine *Regulation*.

In order to maintain its independence, the Cato Institute accepts no government funding. Contributions are received from foundations, corporations, and individuals, and other revenue is generated from the sale of publications. The Institute is a nonprofit, tax-exempt, educational foundation under Section 501(c)3 of the Internal Revenue Code.

CATO INSTITUTE
1000 Massachusetts Ave., N.W.
Washington, D.C. 20001